Veterans

Veterans

Other Books of Related Interest:

Opposing Viewpoints Series
The Armed Forces

At Issue Series
U.S. Military Deployment

Current Controversies Series
Afghanistan

"Congress shall make no law . . . abridging the freedom of speech, or of the press."

First Amendment to the U.S. Constitution

The basic foundation of our democracy is the First Amendment guarantee of freedom of expression. The Opposing Viewpoints Series is dedicated to the concept of this basic freedom and the idea that it is more important to practice it than to enshrine it.

OPPOSING VIEWPOINTS® SERIES

| Veterans

Margaret Haerens, Book Editor

GREENHAVEN PRESS
A part of Gale, Cengage Learning

GALE
CENGAGE Learning™

Detroit • New York • San Francisco • New Haven, Conn • Waterville, Maine • London

12|10   # 607477099

GALE
CENGAGE Learning·

Christine Nasso, *Publisher*
Elizabeth Des Chenes, *Managing Editor*

© 2011 Greenhaven Press, a part of Gale, Cengage Learning.

Gale and Greenhaven Press are registered trademarks used herein under license.

For more information, contact:
Greenhaven Press
27500 Drake Rd.
Farmington Hills, MI 48331-3535
Or you can visit our Internet site at gale.cengage.com

For product information and technology assistance, contact us at

Gale Customer Support, 1-800-877-4253
For permission to use material from this text or product, submit all requests online at www.cengage.com/permissions

Further permissions questions can be emailed to permissionrequest@cengage.com

Articles in Greenhaven Press anthologies are often edited for length to meet page requirements. In addition, original titles of these works are changed to clearly present the main thesis and to explicitly indicate the author's opinion. Every effort is made to ensure that Greenhaven Press accurately reflects the original intent of the authors. Every effort has been made to trace the owners of copyrighted material.

Cover Image copyright © iStockPhoto.com/PinkTag.

LIBRARY OF CONGRESS CATALOGING-IN-PUBLICATION DATA

Veterans / Margaret Haerens, book editor.
    p. cm. -- (Opposing viewpoints)
    Includes bibliographical references and index.
    ISBN 978-0-7377-4994-6 (hardcover) -- ISBN 978-0-7377-4995-3 (pbk.)
    1. Veterans--Services for--United States--Juvenile literature. 2. Veterans--United States--Social conditions--Juvenile literature. 3. United States. Dept. of Veterans Affairs--Juvenile literature. I. Haerens, Margaret.
    UB357.V375 2010
    362.860973--dc22
                                                        2010018885

Printed in the United States of America
1 2 3 4 5 6 7 14 13 12 11 10

Contents

Chapter 3: How Does the VA Address Emerging and Controversial Health Issues?

Chapter 4: How Can the U.S. Government Help Veterans?

Why Consider Opposing Viewpoints?

> *"The only way in which a human being can make some approach to knowing the whole of a subject is by hearing what can be said about it by persons of every variety of opinion and studying all modes in which it can be looked at by every character of mind. No wise man ever acquired his wisdom in any mode but this."*
>
> *John Stuart Mill*

In our media-intensive culture it is not difficult to find differing opinions. Thousands of newspapers and magazines and dozens of radio and television talk shows resound with differing points of view. The difficulty lies in deciding which opinion to agree with and which "experts" seem the most credible. The more inundated we become with differing opinions and claims, the more essential it is to hone critical reading and thinking skills to evaluate these ideas. Opposing Viewpoints books address this problem directly by presenting stimulating debates that can be used to enhance and teach these skills. The varied opinions contained in each book examine many different aspects of a single issue. While examining these conveniently edited opposing views, readers can develop critical thinking skills such as the ability to compare and contrast authors' credibility, facts, argumentation styles, use of persuasive techniques, and other stylistic tools. In short, the Opposing Viewpoints Series is an ideal way to attain the higher-level thinking and reading skills so essential in a culture of diverse and contradictory opinions.

In addition to providing a tool for critical thinking, Opposing Viewpoints books challenge readers to question their own strongly held opinions and assumptions. Most people form their opinions on the basis of upbringing, peer pressure, and personal, cultural, or professional bias. By reading carefully balanced opposing views, readers must directly confront new ideas as well as the opinions of those with whom they disagree. This is not to simplistically argue that everyone who reads opposing views will—or should—change his or her opinion. Instead, the series enhances readers' understanding of their own views by encouraging confrontation with opposing ideas. Careful examination of others' views can lead to the readers' understanding of the logical inconsistencies in their own opinions, perspective on why they hold an opinion, and the consideration of the possibility that their opinion requires further evaluation.

Evaluating Other Opinions

To ensure that this type of examination occurs, Opposing Viewpoints books present all types of opinions. Prominent spokespeople on different sides of each issue as well as well-known professionals from many disciplines challenge the reader. An additional goal of the series is to provide a forum for other, less known, or even unpopular viewpoints. The opinion of an ordinary person who has had to make the decision to cut off life support from a terminally ill relative, for example, may be just as valuable and provide just as much insight as a medical ethicist's professional opinion. The editors have two additional purposes in including these less known views. One, the editors encourage readers to respect others' opinions—even when not enhanced by professional credibility. It is only by reading or listening to and objectively evaluating others' ideas that one can determine whether they are worthy of consideration. Two, the inclusion of such viewpoints encourages the important critical thinking skill of objectively evaluating an author's credentials and bias. This evaluation will illuminate an author's reasons for taking a particular stance on an issue and will aid in readers' evaluation of the author's ideas.

It is our hope that these books will give readers a deeper understanding of the issues debated and an appreciation of the complexity of even seemingly simple issues when good and honest people disagree. This awareness is particularly important in a democratic society such as ours in which people enter into public debate to determine the common good. Those with whom one disagrees should not be regarded as enemies but rather as people whose views deserve careful examination and may shed light on one's own.

Thomas Jefferson once said that "difference of opinion leads to inquiry, and inquiry to truth." Jefferson, a broadly educated man, argued that "if a nation expects to be ignorant and free . . . it expects what never was and never will be." As individuals and as a nation, it is imperative that we consider the opinions of others and examine them with skill and discernment. The Opposing Viewpoints Series is intended to help readers achieve this goal.

David L. Bender and Bruno Leone,
Founders

Introduction

"It's not the powerful weapons that make our military the strongest in the world. It's not the sophisticated systems that make us the most advanced. The true strength of our military lies in the spirit and skill of our men and women in uniform."

—President Barack Obama

While the Department of Veterans Affairs (VA) is busy addressing the needs of millions of U.S. military veterans, it has been dealing with another related challenge: utilizing the newest technology to serve and reach out to as many veterans as possible. The VA strives to provide the most advanced and efficient services to a growing number of veterans. Make no mistake, this is a daunting challenge. The VA is tasked with serving not only the approximately 23.4 million veterans who are currently alive, but also their family members and dependents. All in all, it is estimated that about a quarter of the United States is potentially eligible for VA benefits and services because they are veterans, family members, or survivors of veterans.

For a responsibility of that magnitude, the VA must have adequate resources. As of September 30, 2008, the VA has approximately 278,000 employees, most of which are with the Veterans Health Administration (VHA), a subdepartment of the VA focused on veteran's health care. The VA's health care system includes 153 medical centers, 135 nursing homes, 909 ambulatory care and community-based outpatient clinics, 108 home care programs, and 232 centers for veterans. Almost 5.5 million people received care in VA health care facilities in

2008. Furthermore, to implement technological advances across such a broad and complicated system, a concerted effort must be made and sustained by a group of committed politicians, bureaucrats, and veterans groups.

Experts agree that the VA made a huge step forward in addressing the needs of veterans with the success of the Veterans Health Information Systems and Technology Architecture (VistA). The advantage of VistA is that a VA clinician can call up a comprehensive patient record online, which includes past visits, the patient's medical history, test results, x-rays, and other pertinent data, and then transmit it anywhere. These are called electronic health records (EHRs). Not only did the success of VistA and EHRs significantly decrease cost and errors and increase efficiency, but it also resulted in skyrocketing levels of patient satisfaction. In 2006 the VA was one of the winners of the prestigious Innovations in American Government Award, which rewards government agencies that exhibit innovation in the public sector. Many observers called VistA a model for the broader American health care reform effort, which hopes to make electronic health records a standard part of American health care in the near future.

Advances such as VistA represent major progress in health care record keeping and allow the VA to provide excellent, cost-efficient health care services to veterans. The key to providing services like VistA is funding. Only by securing the funds to adequately design, test, and implement the new technologies and systems that have catapulted VA health care to the forefront of American health care systems can the VA continue its much-needed work. One of the new projects currently in the pipeline is the joint virtual lifetime electronic record, a system to streamline the transfer of medical records between the Department of Defense, which manages the care of active duty servicemen and women, and the VA, which deals with the health care services of military veterans.

For years, funding was a significant problem. In twenty of the last twenty-three years, the U.S. budget did not pass on time, forcing the VA to ration care for the almost 6 million patients who depend on its services. Not only did veterans suffer, but the VA was often left anticipating whether it would have the needed funds for large projects, such as the joint virtual electronic record inititiative. Leading veterans groups fought the funding system, demanding assured funding for the VA to eliminate rationing of care and reimbursement backlogs and to enable the budgeting of new technology, improved services, and revisions of information systems.

Their efforts were eventually rewarded. On October 22, 2009, President Barack Obama signed into law the Veterans Health Care Budget Reform and Transparency Act, which authorizes the U.S. Congress to approve the VA health care budget a year in advance. Veterans groups praised the law, maintaining that the VA could continue to provide a high level of care to its patients while improving current services and seeking out more innovations to keep VA health care one of the U.S. government's most successful programs.

The authors of the viewpoints presented in *Opposing Viewpoints: Veterans* explore the issues and challenges facing veterans and the VA in the following chapters: Are U.S. Military Veterans Being Treated Fairly? What Issues Are Facing the VA? How Does the VA Address Emerging and Controversial Health Issues? How Can the U.S. Government Help Veterans? The information contained in this volume provides insight into some of the recent controversies surrounding the VA and health care for veterans, and it offers some suggestions on how to improve services and outreach to U.S. military veterans.

Are U.S. Military Veterans Being Treated Fairly?

Chapter Preface

In September 2006, the Walter Reed Army Institute of Research published a study on the mental health effects of combat on U.S. military veterans. Its findings were striking. The study reported that of the three hundred thousand soldiers surveyed, one in eight soldiers returning from combat during the first year of the war in Iraq was diagnosed with post-traumatic stress disorder (PTSD) or some other mental illness. More than 19 percent of those soldiers returning from Iraq reported experiencing mental problems. By the end of that first year, 35 percent of Iraq veterans had sought mental health care. The study also found that 12 percent of those seeking help were eventually diagnosed with PTSD, depression, or another serious mental health problem.

The study also reported that soldiers involved in combat situations were more likely to suffer with mental problems. Among the more than twenty-one thousand Iraq veterans who reported suffering from symptoms of PTSD, nearly 80 percent had engaged in combat or had been an eyewitness to combat. According to a 2008 RAND Corporation study, nearly 20 percent of Iraq and Afghanistan veterans are currently experiencing symptoms of PTSD or major depression. However, less than half are getting adequate treatment for their problems.

The Department of Veterans Affairs (VA) offers a variety of programs designed specifically for returning veterans to get help for their mental health problems, including PTSD or depression. Yet, many veterans and their families argue that these programs are of limited value if veterans are not informed about them or cannot access them effectively. Veterans report long wait times for appointments; driving several hours to see a psychiatrist, counselor, or specialist at a VA hospital; or limited appointment slots with VA doctors. Access for veterans living in rural areas is particularly difficult. For the task of reaching out to veterans and providing the best care for complicated and serious mental health issues, soldiers, veterans, veterans groups, and families of veterans give the VA a failing grade.

To its credit, the VA acknowledges that it can be doing a better job and has developed mental health outreach programs to better serve veterans and their families. In 2008 the VA initiated a veterans call center, established to inform soldiers transitioning to civilian life of their benefits, particularly mental health programs that can benefit them. It also created a suicide prevention hotline and publicized it with public service announcements (PSAs) on television, radio, and public transportation. In rural areas, the VA has opened new rural outreach clinics and is launching a program of mobile health care vans and buses. The VA is also utilizing new technologies and social networking sites such as Facebook and Twitter to get the message out about new mental health programs available to those veterans who need them.

The question of whether the VA is adequately reaching out to veterans is one of the issues examined in this chapter. Other topics explored consider the debate over recent Hollywood portrayals of veterans and the important subject of whether American veterans are being treated fairly.

"Just as the Pentagon failed, after its March 2003 invasion of Iraq, to plan for keeping the peace, . . . so has the Veterans Administration failed to plan for caring for casualties of the war."

Veterans Are Not Being Treated Fairly

Judith Coburn

Judith Coburn is a journalist who has written for Mother Jones, Village Voice, *and the* Los Angeles Times. *In the following viewpoint, she contends that the U.S. Congress has underfunded much-needed programs to care for troops returning from Iraq and Afghanistan. Coburn argues that unless budget shortfalls are addressed, the Veterans Administration (VA), the preceding agency of the Department of Veterans Affairs, will not be able to meet the needs of U.S. veterans.*

As you read, consider the following questions:

1. According to the author, how many U.S. veterans have sought treatment from the VA since returning from the Iraq and Afghanistan wars?

2. What percentage of U.S. veterans who served in Iraq have sought treatment from the VA for emotional problems that resulted from their service in the war?

3. What was the budget shortfall in VA funding in the years 2003–2006?

On the eve of his marine unit's assault on Fallujah in November 2004, Blake Miller read to his men from the Bible (John 14:2–3): "In my father's house, there are many mansions: if it were not so, I would have told you. I leave this place and go there to prepare a place for you, so that where I may be, you may be also."

A photograph of Miller's blood-smeared, filthy face, so reminiscent of [American photojournalist] David Douglas Duncan's photos of war-weary marines in Vietnam, is one of the Iraq War's iconic images. Over a hundred newspapers ran it. But as the *San Francisco Chronicle* reported recently, Miller, a decorated war hero, has been shattered psychologically by Iraq. Disabled by flashbacks and nightmares, he continues to pay daily and dearly for his service there.

His eloquent commitment to his fellow marines is the highest value in military life. But the [George W.] Bush administration, which sent Blake Miller, his fellow marines, and 1.3 million other Americans (so far [as of April 2006]) to war in Iraq and Afghanistan apparently does not share this commitment.

A Disappointing Homecoming

Much has been written about how President Bush and Secretary of Defense Donald Rumsfeld waged war on the cheap, sending too few ill-equipped young soldiers—30% of them ill-trained Reservists and National Guardsmen—into battle. But little has been reported about how shockingly on-the-cheap the homecomings of these soldiers have proved to be. The Bush administration awarded Blake Miller a medal, but it has fought for three long years to deny soldiers like him the care they need. While Miller and his men were being thrown into the fire in Fallujah, the White House was proposing to cut the combat pay of soldiers like them. (Only an outburst of outrage across the political spectrum caused the administration to back off from that suggestion.)

The Veterans Administration [VA; currently the Department of Veterans Affairs], now run by a former Republican National Committeeman, has been subjected to the same radical hatcheting that the White House has tried to wield against the rest of America's safety net. Cutbacks, cooking the books, privatization schemes, even a proposal to close down the VA's operations have all been in evidence. The administration's inside-the-beltway supporters like the Heritage Foundation and famed anti-tax radical Grover Norquist like to equate VA care with welfare. Traditionally, however, most Americans have held that the VA's medical care and disability compensation were earned by those who served their country.

Unfortunately, in our draft-free country, the fight to protect the Veterans Administration and to fully fund it has gone on largely out of public sight. Other than the *Washington Post* and the Associated Press, relatively few journalistic organizations have bothered to regularly cover the VA. The fight over it that White House hatchet men, VA political appointees, and their allies in Congress have had with congressional critics (Democratic and Republican) along with veterans organizations has been monitored closely only by veterans Web sites like [columnist] Larry Scott's VAWatchdog.org, veteransfor commonsense.org and military.com.

The Truth About VA Health Care

While national deficits soar, thanks in part to skyrocketing war costs, veterans of Iraq and Afghanistan are flooding into the increasingly underfunded VA system. The Pentagon says that 2,389 Americans have died and 17,648 have been wounded in combat in Iraq (and another 285 have died in Afghanistan). But these casualty figures seem to be significant undercounts. After all, 144,424 American veterans have sought treatment from the VA system since returning from those wars, not including soldiers actually hospitalized in military hospitals.

These figures were wrested only recently from the Veterans Administration after years of fruitless demands from Democrats on the House Committee on Veterans' Affairs. The 144,424 figure includes not only many of those 17,648 reported wounded in combat by the Pentagon—if that figure is, in fact, accurate—but also those wounded psychologically, those injured in accidents, and those whose ailments were caused or exacerbated by service in the war. (Think of war, in this sense, as an extreme sport in its toll on the body.) Of course, neither Pentagon, nor VA figures for the wounded include estimates of those soldiers or veterans who don't show up at a Department of Defense (DoD) or VA facility. Among these casualties are post-combat-tour suicides (who obviously can't show up) and the victims of diseases like leishmaniasis, caused by the ubiquitous sand flies in Iraq, who often suffer on their own.

Nonetheless, the VA has admitted—and it's been confirmed by an Army study—that a staggering 35% of veterans who served in Iraq have already sought treatment in the VA system for emotional problems from the war. Add this to the older veterans, especially from the Vietnam era, pouring into the VA system as their war wounds, both physical and emotional, deepen with age or as, on retirement, they find they can no longer afford private health insurance and realize that VA health care is—or, at least in the past, was—more generous than Medicare.

Just as the Pentagon failed, after its March 2003 invasion of Iraq, to plan for keeping the peace, guarding against looting, fighting a resilient insurgency, or handling a civil war, so has the Veterans Administration failed to plan for caring for casualties of the war. The VA admitted recently that 33,858 more vets showed up for treatment in just the first quarter of FY [fiscal year] 2006 than were expected for the entire year. Do the math yourself. Multiply times 4, assuming that the war goes on injuring Americans at current levels, and you get a possible underestimate of 135,000 casualties for the year.

Even more distressing, the *San Diego Union-Tribune* recently reported that mentally ill soldiers are being sent back to war armed only with antidepressants and antianxiety drugs. The *Union-Tribune* quotes Sydney Hickey of the National Military Family Association as saying that "more than 200,000 prescriptions for the most common antidepressants were written in the last 14 months for service members and their families." According to the *Union-Tribune*, an Army study also found that 17% of combat-seasoned infantrymen suffer from major depression, anxiety, or post-traumatic stress disorder (PTSD) after a single tour in Iraq. California Senator Barbara Boxer has called for an investigation.

Holding the VA Accountable

Are such chronic underestimates merely the result of incompetence? Not according to the Government Accountability Office (GAO), Congress's investigative arm. In a series of reports on the Veterans Administration over the last three years, the GAO found that the VA's top officials submitted budget requests based on cost limits demanded by the White House, not on realistic expectations of how many veterans would actually need medical care or disability support.

In repeated testimony before Congress, top VA political appointees have opposed demands by veterans groups like the American Legion and Disabled American Veterans to increase significantly funds for medical care and disability payments for the new patients now flooding the system. Top VA officials assured Congress that more money wasn't needed because the agency had stepped up "management efficiencies." But the GAO found that, from 2003–2006, there were no obvious management efficiencies whatsoever to offset the increased treatment costs from the Iraq War, nor did the VA even have a methodology for reporting on such alleged efficiencies.

While the GAO's findings, when describing the VA's budget manipulations, were couched in such relatively polite bureaucratic euphemisms as "misleading," "lacked a methodology," and "does not have a reliable basis," the conclusions nonetheless were striking. "The GAO report confirms what everyone has known all along," American Legion National Commander Thomas L. Bock commented. "The VA's health care budget has been built on false claims of 'efficiency' savings, false actuarial assumptions and an inability to collect third-party reimbursements—money owed them. This budget model has turned our veterans into beggars, forced to beg for the medical care they earned and, by law, deserve. These deceptions are especially unconscionable when American men and women are fighting in Iraq and Afghanistan."

Some veterans are calling it fraud. Representative Lane Evans (Dem.-Ill.) of the House Committee on Veterans' Affairs calls it "Enron-styled accounting" [referring to a scandal involving a large energy company's institutional fraud].

Budget Busting

The economic realities of the wars the Bush administration has taken us into are, in truth, budget busting. A recent study by Nobel Prize–winning economist Joseph Stiglitz and Harvard management expert Linda Bilmes—that actually factored the costs of "coming home" into war expenditures—sets the total cost of the Iraq War between $1 and 2 trillion, including $122 billion in disability payments and $92 billion in health care for veterans.

Pentagon health care costs for soldiers still in the military have doubled in the last five years and are projected to total

Veterans Want a Say in Curriculum Planning

A group of . . . veterans and historians is asking the Ohio State Board of Education to delay implementation of new state social studies standards in order to include veterans in curriculum planning.

"After all, the veterans throughout history have created much of that same history, so it only makes good sense to include representatives to participate in the process," said Danny Bare, director of the Clermont County Veterans' Services Commission. . . .

Bare's group thinks history is shortchanged in the nation's and Ohio's schools.

Cindy Kranz,
"Vets Asks to Help Plan Curriculum,"
Cincinnati.com, March 20, 2010.

$64 billion or 12% of the official Pentagon budget by 2015, according to William Winkenwerder Jr., assistant secretary of defense for health affairs.

Soaring American medical costs are only partly to blame. Advances in combat medical care have also meant that far more wounded soldiers are being kept alive than in earlier wars, many of them with serious brain injuries and/or multiple amputations. Taking care of these tragically maimed soldiers for life will be extraordinarily costly, both in terms of medical care and their 100% disability payments. (The VA rates disability on a scale of 0 to 100%, which then determines the size of the monthly disability payment due a veteran.)

Even before recent veterans began flooding the system, the VA was already underfunded and being criticized for poor services. Then, three years ago [in 2003], Rep. Evans and Rep. Chris H. Smith, (Rep.-NJ), chairman of the House Committee on Veterans' Affairs, raised the alarm that the VA, already short of funds, would face a catastrophe as the troops began returning from Iraq.

Exiling the Questioners

Smith was rewarded for his efforts to sound the alarm by being removed not just from his chairmanship, but from the committee altogether, by the House Republican leadership. Similarly, in November 2004, VA head Anthony Principi was forced out by the White House because of his opposition to the VA being shortchanged in the budget the White House demanded—so lobbyists for veterans believe. But Principi seems not to have suffered from his VA experience. The *Los Angeles Times* reported recently that a medical services company Principi headed, and returned to after running the VA, earned over a billion dollars in fees, much of it from contracts approved while Principi was VA chief.

The VA admits its disability system was overburdened even before the administration invaded Iraq; and, by 2004, it had a backlog of 300,000 disability claims. Now, the VA reports that the backlog has reached 540,122. By April 2006, 25% of rating claims took six months to process—no small thing for a veteran wounded badly enough to be unable to work. An appeal of a rejected claim frequently takes years to settle. One hundred twenty-three thousand disability claims have been filed already by veterans of Iraq and Afghanistan. Yet, in its budget requests, the administration has constantly resisted congressional demands to increase the number of VA staffers processing such claims.

The True Cost of Coming Home

Congress has fought the White House over its low VA budgets for several years. In the FY 2006 budget, all Congress could finally grant the VA was $990 million above the agency's already meager request—an increase of just 3.6% over the previous year despite the rise in casualties to be treated. In fact, top VA officials now admit it would take a 14% increase in the present budget simply to keep up with the inflation in medical costs.

Rep. Evans estimates that there has been a $4 billion shortfall in VA funding in the years 2003–06. In 2005, the White House admitted that, for medical services alone, the VA was short $1 billion for the year—and another estimated $2.6 billion in 2006.

What may ultimately swamp the Veterans Administration's ability to cope is the emotional toll of combat—unless it jettisons thousands of returning soldiers. Nearly one in three veterans has been hospitalized at the VA, or visited a VA outpatient clinic, due to an initial diagnosis of a mental health disorder, according to the VA itself. Its numbers are consistent with a recent Army study on soldiers who served in Iraq or Afghanistan. Such a rate might add up over time (depending on how long these wars last) to almost half a million veterans in need of treatment—or more. A 2004 study of several Army and Marine units returning from Iraq and Afghanistan that appeared in the *New England Journal of Medicine* found only 23–40% of those with PTSD had sought treatment. And posttraumatic stress is called "post" for a reason—its most serious symptoms usually emerge long after the trauma is over.

The Bottom Line on PTSD Treatment Costs

Listen to the VA's own national advisory board on PTSD in a report released in February 2006:

> [The] VA cannot meet the ongoing needs of veterans of past deployments while also reaching out to new combat veterans of [Iraq and Afghanistan] and their families within current resources and current models of treatment.

The VA is now paying out $4.3 billion a year for PTSD disability to 215,871 veterans. The report also found that a returning war veteran suffering from emotional illness now has to wait an average of 60 days before he or she can even be evaluated for diagnosis, let alone treated. Forty-two percent of VA primary care clinics had no mental health staff members and 53% of those that did had only one. Eighty-two percent of new patients needed to be in the most intensive PTSD treatment programs, the VA report found, but 40% of those programs were already so full that they could only take a few more patients; 20% said they were too full to take any at all.

"VA's data show a 30% increase in the number of [Iraq and Afghan war] veterans who have an initial diagnosis of post-traumatic stress disorder from the end of FY 2005," says Rep. Michael Michaud (Dem.-Me). "I applaud the courage of these veterans who have sought help, but the administration refuses to acknowledge fully the demand and need for mental health services."

The Emerging Problem of Vet Homelessness and Disability

Further down the line: How many Iraqi veterans will eventually join the ranks of the 400,000 homeless vets on the streets of American cities? (Right now the VA takes care of only 100,000 such vets, according to the National Coalition for Homeless Veterans.)

This dire situation has only encouraged the budget cutters and antigovernment radicals like [Grover] Norquist, who once joked that he hoped to shrink the government enough so that he could drown it in a bathtub. With PTSD rates soaring among vets, the hatchets have been out not just when it comes to treating them, but even when it comes to the diagnosis of PTSD itself. In 2005, the VA, under White House pressure, announced that it was reopening 72,000 long-approved PTSD disability claims for review, many of them for Vietnam veterans. Right-wing columnists quickly swung into action with op-ed pieces insisting that many PTSD claims were fraudulent. The VA backed off—but only after a New Mexico newspaper reported that a troubled Vietnam veteran with a 100% PTSD disability killed himself upon fearing that the VA might review his case and a firestorm of criticism from Congress and veterans organizations followed.

Other White House ideas for cutting back the VA, including making vets pay insurance premiums, higher co-pays and doubling vets' costs for prescription drugs, have also been beaten back by Congress. One VA response to its huge backlog of claims has been to limit enrollment for its services. In January 2003, the White House ordered the VA to create a new temporary cost-cutting category of "affluent" vets who would not be eligible to use the VA. But the new category seems headed for permanency. And it sets the cut-off level for eligibility for VA care so low—around $30,000 for a so-called "affluent" family of four—that many vets who have been cut off can't possibly afford health insurance and medical care on the private market.

In World War II, 12 million Americans fought on behalf of a nation of 130 million. Twenty-five percent of American men served in that war. They came back heroes to a country more than willing to give them the latest medical care, compensate them for their wounds, send them to college, and help them buy homes.

Fifty years later in Iraq—an unpopular war—only 1.3 million are fighting for a nation of 300 million. "Never have so few sacrificed so much for so many," one Desert Storm veteran said recently. Iraq may be the wrong cause for sacrifice. But Vietnam veterans taught us that once war starts we must be willing to take care of everyone who gets hurt in it.

> *"We have only one mission—to care for our nation's veterans, wherever they live, by providing them the highest quality benefits and services possible."*

Veterans Are Offered a Wide Range of Benefits and Services to Help Them in Civilian Life

Eric K. Shinseki

Eric K. Shinseki is a retired four-star general in the U.S. Army and is the U.S. Secretary of Veterans Affairs. In the following viewpoint taken from a speech he gave to the American Legion, he outlines the ways in which the Department of Veterans Affairs (VA) is adjusting to meet the needs of Iraq and Afghanistan war veterans. In particular, he discusses new and continuing VA policies in three key areas: access to medical services, the backlog in medical claims, and homeless veterans.

As you read, consider the following questions:

1. According to Shinseki, how many people work at the VA?

2. How many veterans does Shinseki say there are in the United States?

Eric K. Shinseki, "Remarks to the 91st Annual National Convention of the American Legion," United States Department of Veterans Affairs, August 25, 2009.

3. How many VA medical centers are there across the United States?

Two hundred years ago this past February the 12th [2009], Abraham Lincoln was born here in Kentucky. In his second inaugural address, delivered as the Civil War was drawing to a close, President Lincoln called on our nation "to care for him, who shall have borne the battle and for his widow and his orphan." That charge is as compelling today as it was in 1865. It underscores the uniqueness and vitality of our advocacy on behalf of veterans.

Neither memories nor words can ever repay the debt our nation owes our veterans. Standing at Gettysburg, President Lincoln bore added testimony: "The world will little note nor long remember what we say here, but it can never forget what they did here."

In your day, you earned similar accolades and testimony in Europe and Japan, Korea and Vietnam—in Kuwait and Somalia. On these bloody battlefields, the seeds of American heroism were planted. They are being sown again, today, in Iraq and Afghanistan. It is not just what you did in uniform that is remarkable—it is what you did when you came home that lifted the U.S. from emergent upstart to global superpower. And it was about leadership—your leadership.

Earlier this month [August 2009], we celebrated implementation of the Post-9/11 GI Bill [or the Post-9/11 Veterans Educational Assistance Act, which will provide financial support for education and housing to those who served in the military after the terrorist attacks of September 11, 2001]. Just as you were responsible for passage of the original GI Bill [officially known as the Servicemen's Readjustment Act] of 1944, your commitment was, once again, instrumental in getting this new 9/11 GI bill passed.

The Importance of the American Legion

Returning World War II veterans leveraged the educational opportunity provided by the original GI Bill into sustained economic growth for the nation, catapulting the U.S. to the world's largest economy and, in time, to leadership of the free world. This post-9/11 new GI bill has the potential to impact the country in the same way.

Additionally, you have strengthened our communities through such benchmark initiatives as Boys Nation and Boys State, . . . American Legion Baseball, the National High School Oratorical Contest, and the Heroes to Hometowns program.

Your Operation Comfort Warriors program has raised over $200,000 to buy comfort items and other goods for our wounded service members recovering in VA [Department of Veterans Affairs] and military facilities worldwide.

You have been our eyes and ears in identifying the needs of our service members and veterans, and our conscience for doing what's right. Your military family forum initiative gives the families of service members a chance to voice their concerns, enabling us all to help solve their problems.

Thank you for your continuing service to America. For over 90 years, we have been side by side, and we look forward to continuing this important partnership.

Assessing Veterans' Needs

Over the past seven months, I have visited VA facilities—large and small, urban and rural, complex and simple—all across the country. I've spoken with leaders, staffs, and veterans. I also invited each of our 21 VISN [Veterans Integrated Service Network] directors to share with me their requirements; their priorities; their measurements for performance, quality, and safety; and their need for resources—people, money, and time. I took the final, four-hour VISN presentation two weeks ago. This was time well invested—an invaluable learning experience.

Every day, 288,000 people come to work at VA to serve veterans. We have only one mission—to care for our nation's veterans, wherever they live, by providing them the highest quality benefits and services possible. We must do this faster, better, and more equitably.

The veterans I've met in my travels have been uplifting. Many struggle with conditions inevitable with old age; others live with uncertain consequences from exposures to environmental threats and chemicals; still others have recently returned from Afghanistan and Iraq bearing the fresh wounds of war—visible and invisible.

Out of my encounters with veterans, three concerns kept coming through—access, the backlog, and homeless veterans.

Three Key Concerns

Access. Of the 23.4 million veterans in this country, roughly 8 million are enrolled in VA. Five and a half million have used our medical services at least once; three and a half million visit our medical facilities regularly. Why have over 15 million veterans never enrolled with us? Whatever the reason, VA will continue reaching out to them to explain our benefits, services, and the quality of our health care system.

A major initiative, which will expand access, is the President's [Barack Obama's] decision to welcome back some 500,000 Priority 8 veterans, who lost their entitlements in 2003. We began registering them in July, and we expect 266,000 enrollments this first year, through 2010.

Another initiative to expand and improve access is the evolution of our health care delivery system. VA's 153 medical centers are the flagships of our nationwide integrated health care enterprise. About a decade ago, VA brilliantly decided to move away from the concept of "here are our flagships; come visit us" to one that endeavors to deliver health care to wherever veterans live.

To do that, we have created a system of 768 community-based outpatient clinics, 232 vet centers, outreach and mobile clinics, and when necessary, contracted specialized health care locally.

Our next major leap in health care delivery will be to routinely connect flagship medical centers to distant community-based outpatient clinics and their even more distant mobile counterparts via an IT [information technology] backbone that places specialized health care professionals in direct contact with patients via telehealth and telemedicine hookups.

Today, we are even piloting connectivity from medical centers to the homes of the chronically ill to provide better monitoring and the prevention of avoidable acute episodes. This means that veterans will drive less to receive routine health care, but they will have better access day to day. It will be higher quality and more convenient, especially for veterans challenged by long distances—and prevention will mean healthier lives.

The Backlog of Medical Claims

The backlog. Even though less than 50 percent of the veteran population receives care or benefits from VA, we have a backlog in disability claims. The total number of claims in our inventory today is around 400,000, and backlogged claims that have been in the system for longer than 125 days total roughly 145,000 cases. In July, we closed out 85,000 claims and received another 89,000 new ones. Regardless of how we parse the numbers, there is a backlog; it is too big, and veterans are waiting too long for their checks.

In April, President Obama charged Defense Secretary [Robert] Gates and me to build a fully interoperable electronic records system that will provide each member of our armed forces a virtual lifetime electronic record that will track them from the day they put on the uniform, through their time as veterans, until the day they are laid to rest.

VA is already a leader in the development and use of electronic health records. So is the Department of Defense [DoD]. Between us, DoD and VA have an opportunity to drive the improvement of health care through a fully interoperable electronic health record. Our achievements here may go beyond veterans and service members and could help the nation, as a whole. We are working with the president's chief performance, chief technology, and chief information officers to harness the powers of innovation and technology. For VA, it will revolutionize our claims process—faster processing, higher quality decisions, no lost records, fewer errors. I am personally committed to reducing the processing times of disability claims. We have work to do here, and we have moved out.

A Commitment to Ending Veteran Homelessness

Homelessness. Veterans lead the nation in homelessness, depression, substance abuse, suicides, and they rank up there in joblessness, as well. Here again, this is an accumulation of neglect. We estimate that 131,000 veterans live on the streets of this wealthiest and most powerful nation in the world—men and women, young and old, fully functioning and disabled, from every war generation, even the current operations in Iraq and Afghanistan. Some of them will sleep on the streets here in Louisville tonight.

Six years ago, that number was 195,000, so we think we have the right partners, the right plans, and the right programs in place. We are moving in the right direction to remove this blot on all our consciences.

President Obama and I are committed to ending homelessness among veterans. We are going to take those 131,000 homeless veterans off the streets over the next five years. No one, who has served this nation, as we have, should ever find themselves living without care—and without hope. I know that there are never any absolutes in life, but unless we set an ambitious target, we would not be giving this our very best efforts. To do this well, we will have to attack the entire downward spiral that ends in homelessness—we must offer education, jobs, treat depression, fight substance abuse, and offer safe housing. We have to do it all—no missed opportunities in going from 131,000 to zero and keeping it there—education, jobs, mental health, substance abuse, housing.

Education. The president and senators Jim Webb and John Warner just kicked off our post-9/11 new GI bill program on 3 August. We expect roughly 150,000 veterans to take part in this fully funded, degree-producing program at a state college or university of their choice this year. An additional 1,100 private institutions have elected to participate in a special arrangement called the Yellow Ribbon [GI Education Enhancement] Program. This investment in America's future will go on for decades to come.

The first time we did this in 1944, after World War II, our country ended up being richer by 450,000 trained engineers, 240,000 accountants, 238,000 teachers, 91,000 scientists, 67,000 doctors, 22,000 dentists, and a million other college-educated veterans. They went on to provide the leadership that catapulted our economy to world's largest and our nation to leader of the free world and victor in the Cold War. Lightning is about to strike twice for those who have answered our nation's call.

Valuable Vocational Skills

Jobs. I recently addressed over 1,700 veteran small business owners at the fifth annual small business symposium on 21 July. I reminded them that veterans hire veterans because they know what they're getting. Customers and partners value their skills, knowledge, and attributes and are eager to work with them.

Just last fall, in a survey conducted by the Society for Human Resource Management, over 90 percent of employers said they valued veterans' skills—in particular, their strong sense of responsibility and teamwork.

VA puts veterans first in our contracting awards because we recognize the on-time, on-budget, quality solutions they bring to our contracting needs. In fiscal year 2008, our unique "Veterans First" buying program resulted in VA's spending more than $2 billion on veteran-owned small businesses. That represented 15 percent of our procurement dollars—up 5 percent from the previous year.

During that time, we also doubled our support to service-disabled veteran-owned businesses. That means 12 percent of our procurement dollars—$1.6 billion of $2 billion expended—was invested here.

At VA, our experience is that veteran-owned small businesses have high likelihood for creating new jobs, developing new products and services, and building prosperity. As I said earlier, veterans hire veterans. So increasing opportunities for veteran-owned small businesses is an effective way to help address many needs during this economic downturn.

Protecting the Homeless and Reversing Homelessness

Homeless health care. We will spend $3.2 billion next year to prevent and reduce homelessness among veterans—$2.7 billion on medical services and $500 million on specific homeless programs. With 85 percent of homelessness funding going to health care, it means that homelessness is primarily a health care issue—heavily burdened with depression and substance abuse. The psychological consequences of combat affect every generation of veterans. VA now employs 18,000 mental health professionals to address our mental health needs. We know if we diagnose and treat, people usually get better. If we don't, they won't, and sometimes their problems become debilitating. We understand the stigma issue, but we are not going to be dissuaded. We are not giving up on any of our veterans with mental health challenges, and definitely, not the homeless.

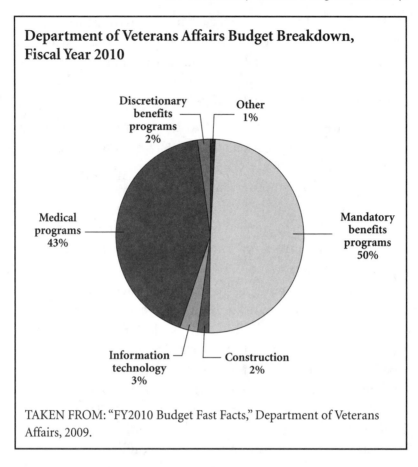

Department of Veterans Affairs Budget Breakdown, Fiscal Year 2010

TAKEN FROM: "FY2010 Budget Fast Facts," Department of Veterans Affairs, 2009.

Homeless housing. We have approximately 500 partners in nearly every major town and city across the country helping us get homeless veterans off the streets. With 20,000 HUD-VASH [Department of Housing and Urban Development and VA Supported Housing] vouchers . . . and our $500 million to invest in 2010, to cover safe housing and rehabilitation for veterans we have been able to coax off the streets, we are going to reduce the number of homeless veterans next year, and each year thereafter, for the next five.

So, education, jobs, health care, and housing: We have work to do here; but we have momentum, and we know where we are headed.

President Obama has charged me with transforming VA into a high-performing 21st-century organization. It will be a different organization from the one that exists today.

Bringing the VA into the 21st Century

Five years from now, we intend to be the provider of choice for more of that larger population of 23.4 million veterans—in insurance, in health care, in education, in home loans, in counseling, and in employment.

To achieve this kind of status with veterans, we must make it easier for them to understand their entitlements and then make it much simpler for them to access their benefits and health care services.

Beyond the five years, we're looking for new ways of thinking and acting. We are asking why, 40 years after Agent Orange [a contaminated herbicide] was last used in Vietnam, this secretary is still adjudicating claims for service-connected disabilities related to it. And why 20 years after Desert Storm, we are still debating the debilitating effects of whatever causes Gulf War illness. Left to our present processes, 20 or 40 years from now, some future secretary could be adjudicating service-connected disabilities from our ongoing conflicts. We must do better, and we will.

If you haven't already heard, the Institute of Medicine recently released a new study on a possible link between Agent Orange and heart disease and Parkinson's [disease]. We have this study under review now, and I assure you—we will get this right.

Any organization our size is bound to have occasional disappointments, and we have not been spared them in recent months. Many of these issues occurred in the past, but I take full responsibility for fixing them. Some of these disappointments resulted from someone cutting corners, while others were failures in leadership, behavior, and professional ethics. And still others were systemic.

Moving Forward on Important Issues

These issues will only be resolved when a sense of responsibility, accountability, and discipline is established throughout VA—from my office to the farthest reaches of our footprint. We are your advocates, and we have begun to retrain the workforce.

My remarks this morning comprise a seven-month progress report on the state of your Department of Veterans Affairs. I intend to do this again next year. Much more remains to be done. We need your continued support and assistance if we are to become the provider of choice. My mission is to serve veterans by increasing their access to our benefits and services, to provide them the highest quality of health care available, and to control costs to the best of my abilities. Doing so will make VA a model of good governance. Doing so will also keep faith with President Lincoln's charge to care for those who have borne the battle and grant them the dignity and respect they deserve until they are laid to rest. That is my mission.

We look for your advice and support in all of these endeavors. Thanks to you, we now have the new Post-9/11 GI Bill. Thanks to you, we also have an agreement with Congress on advance appropriations for VA's three medical accounts. Both the House and the Senate Appropriations Committees have recommended advance appropriations for VA medical care for 2011. I know this has been a priority at American Legion for some time, and I'd like to thank you and the Partnership for Veterans Health Care Budget Reform for your leadership in getting us this far.

Much more remains to be done, and your advice and support continue to be important. For all that you do, you have our deepest respect and thanks.

God bless the men and women who tonight and every other night of the year perform their lonely and demanding missions in the faraway corners of Iraq and Afghanistan. God bless all of you, and God bless our great country.

> *"The facts reflect something very different: Our military men and women are the finest our country has to offer and deserve our thanks and respect each waking moment."*

Recent Hollywood Portrayals of Veterans Are Too Negative

Ben Shapiro

Ben Shapiro is a syndicated conservative columnist and radio host. In the following viewpoint, he accuses Hollywood of offering negative stereotypes of U.S. soldiers and veterans affected by post-traumatic stress disorder (PTSD) and ground down by a cruel military system. He counters that today's films should consider telling stories based on real-life acts of courage of U.S. service members, thereby providing a more true-to-life portrayal of men and women in the U.S. military.

As you read, consider the following questions:

1. What two recent movies does Shapiro feel offer negative stereotypes of U.S. soldiers and veterans?

2. How did U.S. Navy SEAL Michael Monsoor save the lives of two others?

3. How did President George W. Bush eulogize Monsoor?

On Dec. 4, 2009, the radical Hollywood Left is poised to release its latest tribute to the men and women of the armed services, entitled *Brothers*. The film stars Tobey Maguire as a military man serving in Afghanistan. When he is presumed killed in action, his wife, played by Natalie Portman, has an affair with his brother, played by Jake Gyllenhaal. Naturally, Maguire shows up at home with a tremendous case of post-traumatic [stress] disorder—which, if we are to judge from the trailer, causes him to fire weapons at random and physically abuse his wife.

Brothers follows hot on the heels of *The Men Who Stare at Goats*, starring George Clooney, Jeff Bridges and Ewan McGregor. That movie examined the vital issue of military training projects designed to cultivate psychic warriors. Naturally, this involves members of the military looking like morons.

It's no wonder that the mainstream media have labeled the massacre at Fort Hood [on November 5, 2009, in which thirteen were killed] an outgrowth of PTSD [post-traumatic stress disorder] rather than what it is: a terrorist attack by a fifth columnist within the American military. After all, it fits the profile that the Left has for the military: nutty guys with guns who occasionally go postal.

The facts reflect something very different: Our military men and women are the finest our country has to offer and deserve our thanks and respect each waking moment.

A Story Worthy of a Hollywood Movie

If Hollywood wants to tell a story about true American heroes, here's a story:

On Sept. 29, 2006, 25-year-old U.S. Navy SEAL Michael Monsoor was serving in Iraq. As a Navy SEAL, Monsoor was the toughest of the tough. Despite the fact that he was afflicted with asthma, Monsoor became a master-at-arms in the

Stereotypes Are Unfair to Soldiers

Antiwar criticism has morphed into a patronizing attitude toward GIs [members of the military], by way of questioning the quality of the men and women who volunteer to serve. Perhaps it is easier for the antiwar Left to believe that soldiers are unintelligent than to believe that they are taking risks willingly because they actually believe in the war's purpose.

Tim Kane,
"Stupid Soldiers: Central to the Left's Worldview,"
Web Memo #1244, Heritage Foundation, November 3, 2006.

SEALs with expertise in underwater demolitions, parachute training and cold-weather combat. According to the *Los Angeles Times*, Monsoor often led patrols in 100-degree heat while carrying in excess of 100 pounds of gear. Over five months, his platoon killed at least 84 insurgents. In May, Monsoor saved a fellow wounded SEAL, dragging him from a firefight while returning fire one-handed.

But on this day, Sept. 29, Monsoor was stationed atop a building in Ramadi, Iraq, one of the hot spots for fighting terrorists. He was assigned to protect three Navy SEAL snipers. But one of the terrorists got a bead on the outfit and threw a grenade onto the roof. It bounced off Monsoor's chest and fell to the ground. Despite the fact that Monsoor had a clear avenue of escape, he yelled, "Grenade!", then quickly jumped on the grenade, sacrificing his life. By shielding two of his brothers in arms from the grenade with his chest, he saved their lives.

Monsoor's actions eventually won him a posthumous Medal of Honor. President [George W.] Bush broke into tears at the ceremony, even as he praised the fallen hero, stating:

"One of the survivors puts it this way: 'Mikey looked death in the face that day and said, You cannot take my brothers. I will go in their stead.'"

That would be enough of a story. But the real story is what happened at Monsoor's funeral, footage of which can be viewed at YouTube. Almost every Navy SEAL on the West Coast showed up. And as they filed past Monsoor's coffin, each SEAL removed a gold trident, symbolizing membership in the SEAL brotherhood. And then each SEAL slapped his trident into the cherry wood of the coffin, as the echoes reverberated around the silent cemetery. As President Bush described, "The procession went on nearly half an hour. And when it was all over, the simple wooden coffin had become a gold-plated memorial to a hero who will never be forgotten."

Soldiers Deserve Better Treatment

These are our men and women of the United States military. And these are the stories that we must tell about them. They are not victims of some cruel system, ground down into mental dust. They are volunteers for freedom. They stand between us and those who would plunge our nation into darkness.

Where is George Clooney when we need him? Where is Ewan McGregor? Where is Tobey Maguire? Apparently, they are too busy pillorying soldiers as would-be Major Nidal [Malik] Hasans [the shooter at Fort Hood] to remember who our soldiers really are: Michael Monsoors. Heroes. True brothers. And true protectors.

"Recent films about veterans . . . reflect both a desire to honor the soldiers and revulsion toward the atrocities that have occurred."

Recent Hollywood Portrayals of Veterans Are Complex and Inclusive

Tara McKelvey

Tara McKelvey is a senior editor at the American Prospect *and contributing editor at* Marie Claire *as well as a research fellow at New York University School of Law's Center on Law and Security. In the following viewpoint, she asserts that recent films about veterans reflect the ambivalence Americans feel about the reports of soldiers' actions in Iraq and the U.S. involvement in the war. McKelvey argues that the range of cinematic portrayals of veterans reflects the contradictory instinct to honor the soldiers but question the morality and implications of the recent military conflicts.*

As you read, consider the following questions:

1. How many Americans have served in Iraq and Afghanistan and were veterans as of 2008, according to McKelvey?

2. According to McKelvey, what are the three archetypes of veterans portrayed in Hollywood movies?

3. What movie character does McKelvey identify as the ultimate Damaged Hero?

In the 2007 film *In the Valley of Elah*, Vietnam veteran Hank Deerfield is driving to an Army post in New Mexico to look for his son. When he passes a school and notices its American flag is flying upside down, he stops to help an immigrant worker straighten it out and hoist it back up the pole. An upside-down flag is "an international distress signal," explains Deerfield (played by Tommy Lee Jones in an Oscar-nominated role). "It means we're in a whole lot of trouble."

No kidding. Deerfield's son, Mike, has gone absent without leave. Meanwhile, every day across the country, soldiers who have served in the Middle East are fading into the American landscape. Some are resuming their lives, but others—like Mike Deerfield—are finding themselves in lousy, even tragic, circumstances. (The film is loosely based on the murder of a soldier, Richard Davis, in 2003.) *In the Valley of Elah* is one of several new films that chronicle the challenges of the veteran's homecoming. These films include *The Lucky Ones*, released in September; *Red*, about a vet whose dog is killed (released on DVD in October); and Clint Eastwood's *Gran Torino*, which will appear in theaters starting Dec. 17. The latter two may be about Korean War veterans, but all four movies, examined together, reveal the ambivalence that Americans feel about the Iraq War and the men and women who are fighting it.

It is common these days to claim to oppose the war but support the soldiers fighting it. More than 869,000 Americans have served in Iraq and Afghanistan and have since left the armed forces, and civilians are eager to embrace them as ordinary men and women who have sacrificed for their country. Yet the brutal nature of the Iraq War, with the Abu Ghraib scandal, the Haditha killings, and other violent incidents, has raised questions about the actions of individual soldiers and the consequences of the U.S. involvement in Iraq. The new films capture three views of the battle-scarred individual in society—the Good Veteran, the Damaged Hero, and the War Criminal. The Good Veteran has served honorably in wartime and comes home to a society where he is celebrated, more or less, for his sacrifice. The Damaged Hero has also served honorably, but he is treated disrespectfully back in civilian society, and he goes crazy. The War Criminal, a new post-Iraq archetype, has been turned into a torturer by the brutality of the battlefield, and he faces the consequences when he comes home.

The Lucky Ones is about the first kind of veteran—the average working stiff—and it borrows heavily from the 1946 film *The Best Years of Our Lives*. In *Lucky Ones*, three soldiers, Fred Cheever (Tim Robbins), Colee Dunn (Rachel McAdams), and T.K. Poole (Michael Peña), meet for the first time at an airport on their way home from war, just as the characters do in *Best Years*, and travel across America. Dunn walks with a limp, Cheever has broken vertebrae, and Poole, who was hit in the crotch by shrapnel, is worried about his sex life. They drink, fight, and yell at each other, but things never turn particularly violent. When Cheever locks the keys in the car, for example, Dunn and Poole get mad—but not all that worked up. Dunn gets in a bar fight, but the damage is contained. They can cope in the "real world," which is dotted with PetSmart stores and Hummer dealerships, backed by a soundtrack of Sarah McLachlan songs and other music you're likely to hear in Starbucks.

Like the strip-mall landscape, these characters seem to have been expunged of authenticity. They embody the popular wish that decent men and women are fighting the war and that they're all still decent when they return home. They may be bruised by the experience, but things turn out OK because the American public supports them 100 percent. During a blackout at a New York airport, for example, a clerk at a rental car agency says Cheever, Dunn, and Poole can have a car he was saving for his boss, and at a Colorado camp site three sex workers offer to provide discount services. The movie reflects the hope that this country is a place where someone will always reach out to you if you need it—especially if you're a veteran. Whereas in *Best Years* the soldiers show psychological scars of war, in *The Lucky Ones*, bitterness is washed away and replaced by a cheerful, hopeful gloss. In other words, it's a fantasy.

The Damaged Heroes in *Red* and *Gran Torino* have also served honorably in battle, but they have a harder time adjusting to life in America. In *Red*, Avery Ludlow (Brian Cox) is a Korean War vet who goes fishing with his beloved dog. Three teenagers approach him, shake him down for money, and shoot the dog. Ludlow tries to hold the teenagers accountable, turning to the law, the media, and finally his own devices. "I'm after whatever justice can come out of this thing," he explains. Eventually, he shows up at the house of the teenager who killed his dog and brandishes a rifle, demanding that the family acknowledge his loss. Things go downhill from there, culminating in the deaths of two people. In a similar vein, *Gran Torino* features Clint Eastwood as a veteran, Walt Kowalski, who argues with a neighborhood boy who seems intent on stealing his 1972 Ford. Like Ludlow, Kowalski is alienated from society, and he is ready to lash out if he feels he has been wronged.

These films have a cinematic history. The ultimate Damaged Hero is John Rambo, a Green Beret who was turned into

A New Representation of the Modern American Soldier

Much has been made of [the 2010 Oscar-winning film] *The Hurt Locker*'s unending tension and awful beauty. . . . [Its creators] have presented the first accurate portrait of the modern American soldier. Since less than five percent of the American population has served in the military . . . we have had to rely on the media, including Hollywood movies, to form perceptions of the military. Hollywood stereotypes are reductive and often inaccurate, but they are nevertheless powerful touchstones in how America perceives its military. Until *The Hurt Locker*, these perceptions have been formed using seriously outdated models dating back to World War II and the Vietnam War.

Richard Arthur,
"The Hurt Locker: *Beyond Movie Magic*,"
Huffington Post, *March 1, 2010.*

a killing machine in Vietnam and cannot seem to shake his demons in *First Blood* (1982). He comes home and, seven years later, wreaks havoc on the society that created him. This motif also appears in the 1976 film *Taxi Driver*, featuring cabbie-turned-assassin Travis Bickle, who fought in Vietnam. In these movies, veterans are not the easygoing folks seen in *The Lucky Ones*. Instead, they are socially isolated and short-tempered. They are also good at building fires and tend to have body odor. ("He smells like an animal," says a cop, describing Rambo.) Above all, they have a keen sense of justice. "In the field we had a code of honor," says Rambo. "Back here there's nothing." These men settle scores in an amoral, post-war society, and the films reflect an understanding that while violence is sanctioned during war, it may have a spillover effect. These acts are the responsibility of not just the individual soldier but also of society as a whole.

Perhaps the hardest genre of veteran films to watch is that which centers on the War Criminal. In *In the Valley of Elah*, director Paul Haggis (who won an Oscar for 2004's *Crash*) stakes out new filmmaking territory in his attempt to address the moral ambiguity of war. The result is a portrait of a decent guy who goes to war and becomes a torturer, then returns to find a society that, right or wrong, forces him to atone for his misdeeds. In one scene, a detective (Charlize Theron) brushes off Hank Deerfield's request for help in finding his son, Mike, who served for 18 months in Iraq. "He deserves better than this," says Hank. Afterward, Hank tries to find his son in the strip clubs, fast-food joints, and diners of a military town—the opposite of the cheerful, chain-restaurant backdrop in *The Lucky Ones*. The search reveals a series of unpleasant truths as Hank discovers his son was transformed by his experience in Iraq. Mike, having run over an Iraqi child on a road, is consumed with guilt and, later, inflicts pain on wounded detainees. "It became a thing with Mike," a soldier tells his father. "That's how he got the name Doc."

The specter of war crimes has appeared in earlier films such as Oliver Stone's *Born on the Fourth of July*. But in this 1989 movie, the main character, Ron Kovic (Tom Cruise), tries to do the right thing in Vietnam. Kovic is a Damaged Hero—and certainly not a War Criminal. In *In the Valley of Elah*, Mike is an enthusiastic participant in the abuse of detainees. The progression from conscientious soldier to smiling sadist happens quickly and casually, and back home, he is not portrayed as an avenger like Rambo or *Gran Torino*'s Kowalski. He gets his comeuppance.

Taken as a group, the recent films about veterans, ranging from the sunny *The Lucky Ones* to the preternaturally dark *In the Valley of Elah*, seem to suffer from a personality disorder.

They reflect both a desire to honor the soldiers and revulsion toward the atrocities that have occurred. They are an attempt to address widespread contradictions in the perception of the war and its soldiers. *The Lucky Ones* falls short in its portrayal of veterans and how they adjust to civilian society, sugarcoating their experience. *Red* and *Gran Torino* explore some of the darkness of war, showing how it follows soldiers home from the battlefield, and are most successful at portraying one man's experience after combat. *In the Valley of Elah* is the most ambitious, taking on the wrenching subject of torture by Americans and attempting to deal with the moral swamp of the current war. In its attempt to address the war's complexity, the film is disturbing and chaotic—much like America after Iraq.

> *"Despite the fact that the VA's mental health budget has doubled since 2001, ... the VA is still forced to ration care for ... almost 6 million veterans."*

Better Mental Health Outreach Is Needed for Veterans

Reynaldo Leal Jr.

Reynaldo Leal Jr. is a U.S. veteran who is now active with the Iraq and Afghanistan Veterans of America. In the following viewpoint taken from testimony he gave before Congress, Leal describes his harrowing experience suffering from post-traumatic stress disorder (PTSD) and argues that there is not enough mental health outreach for veterans who need it. Leal asserts that with better funding and a better system for stable care, veterans can have critical access to suicide hotlines, regular mental health visits, and adequate family care, among other beneficial services.

As you read, consider the following questions:

1. According to a 2008 RAND study, what percentage of Iraq and Afghanistan veterans are experiencing symptoms of PTSD or major depression?

Reynaldo Leal Jr., Statement Before the House Committee on Veterans' Affairs, House Committe on Veterans' Affairs, May 19, 2009. Reproduced by permission of the author.

2. How many soldiers in Iraq and Afghanistan committed suicide in January 2009, according to the U.S. Army?

3. Leal believes advance funding for the VA can move forward in 2009 thanks to support from what two government entities?

On behalf of Iraq and Afghanistan Veterans of America (IAVA), the nation's first and largest nonpartisan organization for veterans of the current conflicts, I would like to thank you all [the House Committee on Veterans' Affairs] for your unwavering commitment to our nation's veterans.

My name is Reynaldo Leal, and I served in Iraq as a Marine Infantryman with the 3rd Battalion 5th Marines. During my first tour, I participated in some of the Iraq War's heaviest fighting during Operation Phantom Fury in Fallujah, and after that mission was complete, I assisted in securing the first democratic elections in that city. I was deployed for a second time, eight months after my first tour, and conducted counterinsurgency operations along the Euphrates River. As an Infantryman, I did my job well and performed my duties with honor. After my two combat tours, I returned stateside seemingly unscathed, one of only two men in my platoon with that good fortune.

The War at Home

But coming home from war was much harder than I imagined. I was still in the Marine Corps, and I remember being good at our Urban Combat training. Not because I was a natural at it, but because when I began to hear the popping and yelling I felt that I was back in Fallujah. I could feel and see myself fighting the enemy again. It would always take me a while to get back to reality after these training exercises.

When I was discharged from the Marine Corps in February 2008, there were two questions I feared the most: "What was it like over there?" and, "Did you kill anyone?" Anxious about returning home, I delayed going back to south Texas for as long as possible. I couldn't bear the thought of being around familiar faces, and that fear led me to push away those who cared about me the most. As my wife prepared for the birth of our first child, I struggled with flashbacks and painful insomnia, which spiraled into a debilitating depression that alienated my family and threatened my marriage. I knew that my wife was suffering as much as I was and that I wasn't the same person she had fallen in love with. Suicide wasn't an option for me, but every day made me more and more anxious. It turns out I was suffering from a devastating invisible wound: post-traumatic stress disorder (PTSD).

My struggle with PTSD left me dependent on the VA [Department of Veterans Affairs] for mental health care. Since there is no VA hospital close to my home in Edinburg, Texas, I have to either travel five hours each way to the nearest VA hospital in San Antonio or take my chances at our local clinic. The lack of funding for a permanent VA psychologist at this clinic pits me against my fellow veterans for limited appointment slots. If I can't get through on the first of the month to book an appointment, or if both of the psychologist's two daytime slots are full, I'm out of luck until the next month.

Veterans Are Not Getting Adequate Care

Unfortunately, my experience is not unique. According to a 2008 RAND [Corporation] study, nearly 20 percent of Iraq and Afghanistan veterans are experiencing symptoms of PTSD or major depression. But less than half are getting adequate treatment.

PTSD is the silent killer for this generation of veterans. Left untreated, it has the potential to destroy marriages, careers and, in far too many cases, lives. In January of this year [2009], the U.S. Army reported that 24 soldiers in Iraq and Afghanistan committed suicide; a figure that surpassed all combat deaths in those two theaters combined. That alarming

© 2008 Keef, The *Denver Post* and PoliticalCartoons.com.

statistic does not include other branches of services like the Marines, or veterans who have already come home from the war.

But the numbers and statistics are only part of the picture. This new generation of veterans is being left to fend for themselves because of an antiquated system that cannot seem to find a way to reach out to them. There aren't any visible outreach campaigns to get these young men and women through the door of their local VA facility. If they don't know about their benefits, or even where their clinic or hospital is, how can they get the help they need?

VA Needs Better Outreach

When I was struggling with PTSD, there was never a sense that the VA was trying to reach out to me or that anyone even understood. For me, there was the Corps and then there was nothing. One day I had the best health care and support system available for both me and my family, and the next day it was gone. I felt that I had been abandoned and that the fact that I had served my country honorably meant nothing. I didn't know about the claims system, I didn't know about the five years of medical care for Iraq and Afghanistan veterans, and I didn't know that there were others that were going through the same situations that I was. It wasn't until I saw IAVA's "Alone" ad on television and joined Community of Veterans that I felt someone was trying to reach out to me.

It is the responsibility of the federal government and the Department of Veterans Affairs to make sure every veteran feels this way. But are we doing everything we can to reach out to the veterans who have done so much for us? The VA has taken some important steps, especially setting up a suicide hotline, but the answer is no.

We owe it to our veterans to provide the best mental health resources available, and currently we are falling far too short of that goal. At my VA hospital in San Antonio, the psychologist only works two days a week because that Texas clinic, like many VA clinics and hospitals throughout the country, has to stretch its funding to make sure the money lasts the whole year. They don't know how much funding they'll have next year because the VA budget is routinely passed late. In fact, in 19 of the past 22 years, the budget has not been passed on time.

So despite the fact that the VA's mental health budget has doubled since 2001, thanks to the dedication of veterans supporters in Congress, the VA is still forced to ration care for the almost 6 million veterans that depend on its services.

Give VA the Funds It Needs

By fully funding the VA health care budget one year in advance, we could provide a simple solution that would help give VA hospitals and clinics across the country the ability to provide stable care for decades to come. With the ability to plan ahead, these hospitals and clinics could meet critical staffing and equipment needs, so that veterans like me are not left waiting. President [Barack] Obama recently reiterated his support for advance funding of VA health care, and we were glad to hear it. With the strong support of the president and bipartisan leadership of Congress, advance funding can and must move forward this year.

Real action cannot come at a more critical time. As we saw just last week [May 11, 2009] with the tragic events at Camp Liberty [in which an American soldier killed five fellow soldiers at a clinic], our service men and women are under incredible strain. As a nation, we must have the same emphasis on giving our veterans the necessary tools to readjust to civilian life as we have in giving them the tools to survive in combat.

Make no mistake about it, the veterans of this country want nothing more than to become successful and productive members of the society we fought so hard to defend.

> *"We applaud all that has been done to date. While commendable, we can [do] better and should do more."*

Veterans Outreach Is Improving

Richard A. Jones

Richard A. Jones is the legislative director of the National Association for Uniformed Services. In the following viewpoint taken from testimony given before Congress, Jones investigates the effectiveness of the outreach efforts of the Department of Veterans Affairs (VA) to inform U.S. veterans about expansion and changes in VA health care services. Jones concludes that although outreach programs are improving—including efforts to reach more veterans in rural areas as well as those with mental health issues—there are still a number of areas that need more attention.

As you read, consider the following questions:

1. How many Iraq and Afghanistan veterans have used VA health care through 2008?

2. What is Public Law 110-329?

Richard A. Jones, "U.S. Department of Veterans Affairs Medical Care: The Crown Jewel and Best-Kept Secret," Statement Before the House Committee on Veterans' Affairs, U.S. Department of Veterans Affairs, May 19, 2009. Reproduced by permission of the author.

3. By 2013, how many additional veterans will gain access to VA services?

The National Association for Uniformed Services [NAUS] celebrates its 41st year [in 2009] in representing all ranks, branches and components of uniformed services personnel, their spouses and survivors. NAUS membership includes all personnel of the active, retired, Reserve and National Guard, veterans community and their families. We also serve as the main contact for the Society of Military Widows, a support organization for women whose husbands died in military service or in retirement. We support our troops, honor their service, and remember our veterans, their families and their survivors.

It is well known that the Department of Veterans Affairs [VA] Veterans Health Administration (VHA) is the largest provider of health care in the nation. Approximately 6 million veterans annually come to VHA for all or part of their personal health care.

As we take a measure of satisfaction in the quality of care provided at VHA hospitals and clinics, it is important to recognize that many veterans continue to view VA care through the eyes of a past era when VA care was subpar, or in some instances not realizing that the system is available to them.

Assessing the VA System

While we can never fully repay those who have stood in harm's way, a grateful nation has a duty and obligation to provide benefits and health care to its veterans as a measure of its share of the costs of war and national defense.

As the National Association for Uniformed Services assesses the effectiveness of VHA outreach, we believe it is important that we first have an understanding on the number of OEF/OIF [Operation Enduring Freedom in Afghanistan/ Operation Iraqi Freedom] troops using the department's health care system.

At present, nearly 2.0 million troops have served in the two theaters of operation since the beginning of the conflicts in Iraq and Afghanistan. In addition, with the drawdown of troops from the battlefields of Iraq, VA is likely to face increased enrollment.

Through the last quarter of fiscal year 2008, 400,304 separated Operation Enduring Freedom and Operation Iraqi Freedom veterans have used VA health care. And with passage of Public Law 110-329, VA will develop provisions for expanded enrollment for certain Priority 8 [the lowest level on the VA priority list] veterans.

In fact, the final rule for the regulation of accepting these newly eligible veterans is June 15, 2009, which is just around the corner.

Expansion of Priority 8 Veterans

Public Law 110-329 provides funding to allow an approximate 10 percent expansion on the numbers of Priority 8 veterans enrolled and treated at VA medical facilities. The proposed regulations were published in the *Federal Register* on Jan. 21, 2009, and are expected to be finalized by mid-June.

Eligibility will be based upon means testing and will be geographically based to allow for the variances in cost of living in the various regions of the country.

VA expects approximately 266,000 additional Priority 8 veterans to be enrolled in FY [fiscal year] 2010. We are pleased to hear the VA's undersecretary for health state that Priority 8 enrollment is not capped. Any veteran who meets the requirement will be enrolled in the VA health care system. We applaud the effort to end the enrollment ban on veterans.

The budget submission provides more funding to continue this expansion so that by fiscal year 2013 an additional 500,000 qualified veterans will gain access to VA.

Although not specifically addressed in the budget, we would hope that part of the funding for outreach would be used to ensure that everything possible is done to bring awareness of the change in policy to those newly qualified veterans.

VA Needs to Spread the Word

The National Association for Uniformed Services is concerned that well-meaning intentions of the VA might not be enough to spread the word on the expansion of benefits to veterans who have been denied VA medical access for over six years.

Many Priority 8 veterans tried to enroll after the January 17, 2003, prohibition and were denied, therefore, access to VHA care. We believe that the VA plan to mail all individuals previously denied enrollment is a good first step. We are hopeful that there will be follow-up to make sure measures are taken to contact those veterans. Enrolling those qualified veterans who desire to do so into the VA medical system should be a very high priority.

In addition, we must ensure that all veterans returning from combat areas are aware of, and if possible, already signed up for, their five years of VA medical care. Both of these sets of veterans need to be aware of their benefits.

We do recognize, however, that some long-term health conditions, such as post-traumatic stress disorder or traumatic brain injury, may not manifest conditions until many years later. Therefore we encourage further opening of access to sick and disabled veterans beyond the current five-year allowance.

Of course, veteran and military service organizations will gladly help spread the word to their memberships and others. That way we can, together, be better assured that more veterans will be advised of the changes.

VA Budget Outreach Initiatives

The National Association for Uniformed Services is encouraged that the fiscal year 2010 veterans' budget request has numerous outreach programs that will help get the message about VHA to many more veterans and survivors.

These initiatives include reaching out to veterans who live in rural areas of America. The funding requested would allow the VA to more aggressively reach out to these veterans and to possibly set up additional rural outreach clinics to help reach our National Guard and Reserve troops. There is also funding requested for more aggressive tactics to reach those who have mental health issues with expansions of outreach services at veterans clinics.

The budget also includes additional funding for outreach by the newly created Office of Survivors Assistance (OSA) to help serve the numerous survivors who may not have the information on benefits they may be entitled to or apply for.

Advancement in Battlefield Medicine

As is well known, advancement in battlefield medicine has improved the chances of survival in warfare. However, many of our present-day wartime casualties suffer from multiple severe injuries such as amputation, traumatic brain injury (TBI) and post-traumatic stress disorder (PTSD). Care for these individuals requires an intense management of treatment for their injuries and special consideration of their families who stand by these returning heroes.

Reports from VA indicate that, from fiscal year 2002 through the end of 2008, 39 percent (325,000) of the total separated OEF/OIF veterans have obtained VA health care. Among this group, 96 percent were evaluated and [have] been seen as outpatients only, not hospitalized. The remaining 4 percent (13,000) OEF/OIF patients have been hospitalized at least once in a VA health care facility.

Last year, VA informed the National Association for Uniformed Services that of the OEF/OIF veterans who have sought VA health care, approximately 166,000 were former active duty troops and 159,000 were Reserve and National Guard members. The population seeking care is nearly half active duty and half Reserve Component troops.

In total, over the last six years VA reports that 6 percent of the 5.5 million veterans in the VA medical care system are veterans of the most recent military conflict, OEF/OIF veterans.

Relevant Factors in the Health Care Usage Rate

The department attributes the rate of VA health care used by recent veterans to two major factors. First, the department says that recent combat veterans have ready access to the VA system, which is free of charge for five years following separation. In addition, the department attributes that a high rate of veteran participation is due to an extensive outreach effort developed by VA to inform veterans of their benefits, including "a personal letter from the VA secretary to war veterans identified by DoD [Department of Defense] when they separate from active duty and become eligible for VA benefits."

The National Association for Uniformed Services applauds efforts under the direction of the department to establish a dedicated outreach program directed at nearly 570,000 Afghanistan and Iraq combat veterans. The effort, according to VA, is to make sure these veterans are aware of VA's medical services and other benefits for which they are entitled.

The VA outreach program targets OEF/OIF veterans who have been separated from military service but have not sought VA care or services. We encourage the VA health care community to continue its efforts to inform veterans and their families, as well as the medical community, about the availability of VA health care.

The National Association for Uniformed Services asks VA that it leave no stone unturned to reach these veterans.

In examining the effectiveness of the outreach effort, it is important to recognize the stark difference in today's VA's efforts compared to those used in the recent past several years.

Outreach Has Improved, but VA Can Still Do Better

While we commend the positive change in expression and tone, we remain attentive to see that the most recent effort and the improved tone it reflects does not fail. Clearly, there are concerns. Though the system is clearly no longer our grandfather's VA system, negative residue from a previous more closed-minded attitude remains within the system.

Last year, for instance, we received callous reports about a message issued from a VA medical center in Temple, Texas, that suggested time and money could be saved if diagnosis of PTSD were stopped or deeply discounted in its degree of severity.

A PTSD program coordinator and psychologist at the Olin E. Teague Veterans Center sent an e-mail with the subject line "Suggestion" to several VA staffers working with PTSD cases. The e-mail suggested that VA doctors and clinicians give altered diagnosis to patents exhibiting symptoms of PTSD in order to save time and money. In the e-mail, the staffer said, "We really don't . . . have time to do the extensive testing that should be done to determine PTSD."

While VA has long since repudiated the wrong-headed message, it does represent a concern we all should share, namely that VA care may be arbitrary, directed more by budget considerations than the consideration of the treatment necessary for the health of the men and women who served in the armed forces.

The incident is deeply troubling because veterans not only need to hear about the services they earned and deserve; they also need to know that once they come to VA their exams are completed and their services are delivered. . . .

Awareness of Services

As we head toward Memorial Day next week, your subcommittee [the House Committee on Veterans' Affairs] takes a

A Medical Center for Veterans Expands

Christopher McGurk, a U.S. Army veteran from Belchertown [Massachusetts] who served in Iraq and Afghanistan, is a state outreach coordinator in the Statewide Advocacy for Veterans' Empowerment, or SAVE, program. He said he's probably steered about 15 area veterans to services at the VA [Department of Veterans Affairs] Medical Center in Leeds during the past six months. But most of those veterans served in Vietnam, not the more recent conflicts in Iraq and Afghanistan, he noted.

"A lot of them still won't admit that they need help," McGurk said, of the younger generation of returning combat veterans. . . . "It's kind of difficult to broach the subject of mental health treatment when they don't want to hear it."

In recent years, the medical center has significantly increased the number of psychologists, social workers and others who provide veterans with mental health services. A staff of 50 people four years ago [in 2005] has mushroomed to more than 90 inpatient and outpatient mental health workers at the Leeds facility and its satellite clinics today.

Dan Crowley,
"Expanding VA Adjusts to Needs of Returning Veterans,"
Gazettenet.com, December 11, 2009.

good, well-traveled road. In sending young men and women to defend our nation, it is important that we let them know what our great and generous country provides them following their service. Indeed, it is critical.

It is clear to the National Association for Uniformed Services that veterans are generally more aware about the availability of benefits and services than they were four to six years ago. But the value of timely, reliable outreach programs cannot be understated.

Six years ago, for instance, the administration was deeply opposed to spending resources aimed at making veterans aware of the benefits and services available at the Veterans [Affairs] Department. And facilities were in decline.

At one point in that past period, a former secretary of veterans affairs told the nation that the department budget was adequate. "Not a nickel more is needed," he said. However, only a month later the secretary reversed his statement to tell the nation that his department would fall $1.5 billion short of the resources needed to carry veterans services through the remainder of the year.

Prior to this revelation, the National Association for Uniformed Services and other associations had presented ample witness to deficiencies throughout the system. We pleaded with Congress and the administration that funding levels were totally inadequate and, if not addressed, would lead to critical reductions in the availability of veterans health care services, cuts in veterans education benefits, and logjams in veterans disability claims for service-connected injury or illness.

A Low Point for the VA

During that period, things were so bad that a memorandum sent out by the deputy undersecretary for operations and management (July 19, 2002) actually directed all of its health care providers to stop marketing VA programs to veterans.

In basic, the July 2002 memo said too many veterans were coming in for services and VA was spending too much money. It directed VA officials across the country to "stop outreach to veterans." VA employees were directed to stop participating in VA health fairs, stand-downs and related outreach events that informed veterans about programs available to them. Medical facilities were prohibited even from putting out newsletters informing veterans about the services they were legally entitled to receive.

We are thankful that we are beyond that deeply troubling period. If similar incompetence were in place today, many of OEF/OIF veterans would struggle alone with their symptoms and illnesses following deployment.

Stress and the Risk of Health Issues

Studies conducted by the army surgeon general's Mental Health Advisory Team clearly show that our troops and their families face incredible stress today. According to the Department of Defense (DoD), 27 percent of noncommissioned officers on their third or fourth tour exhibited symptoms commonly referred to as post-traumatic stress disorder. That figure is far higher than the roughly 12 percent who show those symptoms after one tour and the 18.5 percent who demonstrate these disorders after a second tour.

And among the approximately half-million active-duty soldiers who have served in Iraq, more than 197,000 have deployed more than once, and more than 53,000 have deployed three or more times.

A recent RAND Corporation study suggests that almost half of these returning troops will not seek treatment. Many of these veterans do not believe they are at risk or they fear that admitting to a mental health problem will mean being stigmatized. Yet if these brave individuals and their families are made aware of access to VA facilities, to which they are entitled, they are likely to find a treatment therapy that leads to [better] health.

If not addressed, stress symptoms can compound and lead to more serious health consequences in the future.

Congress Champions Resources for VA

Recent congressional successes in provided increases in VA spending present the department with an opportunity to advance an awareness of VHA accessibility and readiness to meet health care needs.

We applaud all that has been done to date. While commendable, we can [do] better and should do more. In some cases, a successful outreach can be a matter [of] life and death. Veterans need to hear that VA is part of our nation's commitment to them. They need to hear that with appropriate care, our veterans can tackle stress and get themselves back on track.

NAUS believes that your interest in targeting information to veterans marks a turning point in outreach efforts. We are optimistic. But it is clear that more needs to be done, including follow-through throughout the VA system, within the veterans community and in our educational assistance programs.

We Have a Responsibility to Veterans

Of course, there is a financial cost to improved outreach. But as important is the fact that if we do not make veterans aware of the benefits and services available to them, there is a hidden cost in lives lost, families disrupted and long suffering in homelessness and related problems for decades to come.

We urge the subcommittee to continue its excellent work with other champions in this Congress to ensure resources are ready not only for the provision of a veteran's earned benefits but also for the veteran's awareness of these services as well. It is important that we do so. After all, these brave men and women shouldered a rifle and risked everything to accomplish their mission, to protect another people's freedom and our own country from harm.

As a nation, we need to understand that the value of their service is far greater than the price we pay for their benefits and services.

As a staunch advocate for veterans, the National Association for Uniformed Services recognizes that these brave men and women did not fail us in their service to our country. They did all our country asked and more. Our responsibility is clear. We must uphold our promises and provide the benefits they *earned* through honorable military service.

Periodical Bibliography

The following articles have been selected to supplement the diverse views presented in this chapter.

Julian E. Barnes, Ned Parker, and John Horn — *"The Hurt Locker* Sets Off Conflict," *Los Angeles Times*, February 25, 2010.

Christian Davenport — "Some Iraq, Afghanistan War Veterans Criticize Movie *Hurt Locker* as Inaccurate," *Washington Post*, February 28, 2010.

Tom Donnelly — "They're Warriors, Not Victims," *Weekly Standard*, February 27, 2009.

Elizabeth Franklin — "The Emerging Needs of Veterans: A Call to Action for the Social Work Profession," *Health & Social Work*, August 1, 2009.

Joe Klein — "Giving Back to Veterans," *Time*, July 3, 2008.

Dahlia Lithwick — "A Separate Peace," *Newsweek*, February 11, 2010.

James Ridgeway — "The Veteran Suicides," *Mother Jones*, November 11, 2009.

Steve Russell — "On the Edge?" *Weekly Standard*, February 15, 2008.

Jim Stevenson — "Helping Vets Get Their Well-Earned Benefits," *Policy & Practice*, August 2009.

CHAPTER 2

What Issues Are Facing the VA?

Chapter Preface

The role of women in the U.S. military has been evolving. Back in the days of the Revolutionary War, women participated as soldiers, cooks, laundresses, spies, and nurses in unofficial capacities, performing vital support services to American troops. Women again carried out these services in the Civil War and in the Spanish-American War. In the early twentieth century, the military recognized the necessity of establishing and maintaining a permanent women's nursing corps in the army and the navy. When the U.S. joined World War I in 1917, women had an official role in fighting for their country as army and navy nurses. They were also enlisted in support capacities in the navy, Marine Corps, and the Coast Guard. However, their numbers were limited and most participated in the war as civilian volunteers.

It was World War II that opened the floodgates for women in the military forces. Women were allowed to enroll and fill jobs ranging from clerical to intelligence to piloting efforts. By the end of the war, women were accepted as valuable soldiers who fulfilled an essential role in the war effort and were welcomed in every service branch. They served overseas as well as at home and earned Purple Hearts, Bronze Star Medals, and Legions of Merit for their services. It has been estimated that more than four hundred thousand women served in World War II. In 1948 President Harry S. Truman responded to this impressive contribution by signing the Women's Armed Services Integration Act of 1948, which established a permanent role for women in the U.S. military forces. However, instead of offering women advanced opportunities to serve their country, they placed them only in traditionally female roles, such as clerical, nursing, and administrative jobs.

This regressive state of affairs lasted until the 1970s, when a switch to an all-volunteer force and a concerted challenge to the military's policies of sexual discrimination began to open up opportunities for women once again. Reserve Officers' Training Corps (ROTC) programs became coeducational. By 1976 one out of thirteen military recruits was a woman. That same year, women were accepted into the military services academies. However, it wasn't until 1990 and operations Desert Shield and Desert Storm that female soldiers were on the frontlines in combat, often in leadership roles. By the middle of the 1990s, Congress finally repealed the last restrictions on women's services, except for a few occupational fields.

Today women make up about 20 percent of the U.S. military, with approximately 212,000 women serving in active duty. More than 1 million military veterans are women. As more and more women leave active duty, they will be joining the ranks of military veterans and will require veterans services including health care, employment and vocational services, and educational benefits.

Whether the Department of Veterans Affairs (VA) can handle the growing number of female veterans is just one of the issues explored in this chapter, which considers several of the key challenges the VA faces in the twenty-first century. Other viewpoints examine the VA's performance in relation to Iraq and Afghanistan veterans as well as older veterans suffering from Gulf War illness.

"As the Iraq war approaches its fourth anniversary, the Department of Veterans Affairs is buckling under a growing volume of disability claims and rising demand for medical attention."

The VA Is Ill-Prepared to Meet the Influx of Iraq and Afghanistan War Veterans

Linda Bilmes

Linda Bilmes teaches at the John F. Kennedy School of Government at Harvard University, and she is co-author of the report The Economic Costs of the Iraq War. *In the following viewpoint, she argues that the George W. Bush administration didn't plan on the exploding number of veterans who would need medical and disability care. Bilmes urges Congress to allocate more funding to allow the Department of Veterans Affairs (VA) to accommodate the growing number of claims.*

As you read, consider the following questions:

1. For every one fatality in Iraq, there are how many injuries, according to Bilmes?

Linda Bilmes, "The Battle of the Wounded," *Los Angeles Times*, January 5, 2007. Reproduced by permission of the author.

2. As of 2007, about how many Iraq and Afghanistan veterans have been treated at VA medical facilities?

3. According to the author, how many veterans have the popular Vet Centers treated?

The new year [2007] brought with it the 3,000th American death in Iraq. But what's equally alarming—and far less well known—is that for every fatality in Iraq, there are 16 injuries. That's an unprecedented casualty level. In the Vietnam and Korean wars, by contrast, there were fewer than three people wounded for each fatality. In World Wars I and II, there were less than two.

That means we now have more than 50,000 wounded Iraq war soldiers. In one sense, this reflects positive change: Better medical care and stronger body armor are enabling many more soldiers to survive injuries that might have led, in earlier generations, to death. But like so much else about this war, the [George W.] Bush administration failed to foresee what it would mean [and] failed to plan for the growing tide of veterans who would be in urgent need of medical and disability care. The result is that as the Iraq war approaches its fourth anniversary, the Department of Veterans Affairs [VA] is buckling under a growing volume of disability claims and rising demand for medical attention.

So far, more than 200,000 veterans from Iraq and Afghanistan have been treated at VA medical facilities—three times what the VA projected, according to a Government Accountability Office analysis. More than one-third of them have been diagnosed with mental health conditions, including post-traumatic stress disorder, acute depression and substance abuse. Thousands more have crippling disabilities such as brain or spinal injuries. In each of the last two years, the VA has underestimated the number of veterans who would seek help and the cost of treating them—forcing it to go cap in hand to Congress for billions of dollars in emergency funding.

Forces Deployed to Iraq and Afghanistan by Service (as of June 2008)

	Total active duty strength	Total deployed to Iraq (percent of total forces)	Total deployed to Afghanistan (percent of total forces)	Average length of deployment
Defense Department (total)	1,385,122 (100%)	183,100 (100%)	31,700 (100%)	
Army	531,526 (38)	117,100 (64)	21,700 (68)	12 months
Navy	331,785 (24)	20,800 (11)	1,300 (4)	5 months
Marine Corps	193,040 (14)	24,500 (13)	3,600 (11)	8 months
Air Force	328,771 (24)	20,700 (11)	5,100 (16)	4 months

TAKEN FROM: Lawrence J. Korb, Peter M. Juul, Laura Conley, Major Myles B. Caggins III, and Sean E. Duggan, "Building a Military for the 21st Century: New Realities, New Priorities," Center for American Progress, December 2008.

Strain Is Showing

The VA system has a reputation for high-quality care, but waiting lists to see a doctor at some facilities now run as long as several months. Shortages are particularly acute in mental health care. Dr. Frances Murphy, the VA's deputy undersecretary for health, recently wrote that some VA clinics do not provide mental health or substance abuse care, or if they do, "waiting lists render that care virtually inaccessible."

The VA also runs Vet Centers—207 walk-in neighborhood help centers that provide counseling to veterans and their families. These popular, low-cost centers have already treated 144,000 new veterans. But they are so understaffed that nearly half are sending veterans who need individual therapy into group sessions or placing them on waiting lists, according to a recent report by the House Committee on Veterans' Affairs.

At the same time, wounded veterans trying to obtain disability checks are being tied up in a bureaucratic nightmare. The Veterans Benefits Administration has a backlog of 400,000 pending claims—and rising. Veterans must wait from six months to two years to begin receiving the money that is due to them while the agency plods through paperwork. The staff eventually helps veterans secure 88% of the benefits they ask for—but in the interim, thousands of veterans with disabilities are left to fend for themselves.

The Situation Will Get Worse

The situation is about to go from bad to worse. Of the 1.4 million service members involved in the war effort from the beginning, 900,000 are still deployed on active duty. Once they are discharged, the demands for medical care and counseling will skyrocket, as will the number of benefit claims. The Veterans for America organization projects that VA medical centers may need to treat up to 750,000 more returning Iraq and Afghan war veterans and that half a million veterans may visit the Vet Centers.

And then there is the cost. After the Persian Gulf War in 1991, half of all veterans sought VA medical care, and 44% filed disability claims. Assuming that this pattern is repeated, the lifetime cost of providing disability payments and health care to Iraq and Afghan war veterans will likely cost U.S. taxpayers between $300 billion and $600 billion, depending on how long the war lasts.

President Bush is now talking about spending more money on recruiting in order to boost the size of the army and deploy more troops to Iraq. But what about taking care of those soldiers when they return home? The VA's solution is to hire an additional 1,000 claims adjudicators to cut the backlog.

Support VA Funding Increases

A better idea would be to stop examining each application and instead automatically accept all disability claims, then audit a sample (like the IRS [Internal Revenue Service] does for tax filings) to weed out fraud. Or at a minimum, simple claims should be fast-tracked and settled within 60 days. We should also place more counselors and more claims experts in the Vet Centers and harmonize record keeping so veterans can move seamlessly from the army's payroll into VA hospitals and outpatient care.

One of the first votes facing the new Democratic-controlled Congress will be another "supplemental" budget request for $100 billion-plus to keep the war going. The last Congress approved a dozen such requests with barely a peep, afraid of "not supporting our troops." If the new Congress really wants to support our troops, it should start by spending a few more pennies on the ones who have already fought and come home.

> *"Every day, 288,000 people come to work at VA [Department of Veterans Affairs] trying to do the right thing, serving veterans to the best of their ability."*

The VA Is Preparing to Meet the Needs of Iraq and Afghanistan War Veterans

Jose Riojas

Jose Riojas is the assistant secretary of the Department of Veterans Affairs (VA). In the following viewpoint, he acknowledges that the VA has not been performing to the level of a modern organization in recent years and outlines the changes planned to bring veterans services in line with modern technology to serve the changing demographics of today's veterans. Riojas reaffirms the VA's commitment to providing the best services—educational, vocational, medical, psychological, and financial—for U.S. military veterans.

As you read, consider the following questions:

1. What does Riojas cite as the three VA principles that must be met by a trained and capable workforce?

Jose Riojas, "Remarks by Assistant Secretary Jose Riojas at the Vietnam Vetrans of America 2009 National Convention," US Department of Veterans Affairs, 2009.

2. How many veterans does the VA want to get into college under the new GI bill by fall 2009?

3. How does the VA plan to update the electronic records system to help veterans?

Every day, 288,000 people come to work at VA [Department of Veterans Affairs] trying to do the right thing, serving veterans to the best of their ability. Of course, any organization our size will have problems, and we've had our share in recent years. Some can be traced to a single individual cutting corners. But others are failures of management or leadership, and some are fundamentally systemic.

I think we can all agree that VA is not performing up to the level of a modern high-tech organization. In response to that concern, President [Barack] Obama has charged Secretary [Eric K.] Shinseki with transforming VA into the high-performing 21st-century organization, an organization adapted to new realities, leveraging new technologies to serve the new demographics of today's veterans with renewed commitment.

People ask, "Where do you want to be five years from now?" The answer is: We want to be the provider of choice for veterans—for life insurance, for medical care, for education, for home loans, for counseling, and for employment.

We want to be the veteran's first choice for each of these, offering the best product and the best service available. We already offer many of the best products. Where we need the most improvement is on the service side. We need to make it easier for veterans to find out about their benefits, and easier for them to access those benefits.

How do we do that?

A Long-Term Leadership Challenge

The change envisioned can only be accomplished through determined leadership, so we've begun to put in place a first-rate leadership team that's both reflective of the veterans we serve and committed to the mission of transformation.

A New Bill Will Support Returning Veterans

More college-educated professionals will enter the next generation's professional workforce as a result of the Post-9/11 GI Bill [Post-9/11 Veterans Educational Assistance Act], Veterans Affairs [VA] Secretary Eric K. Shinseki said this week [in August 2009] at the American Legion's 91st National Convention in Louisville, Ky.

Shinseki lauded the organization's efforts in advocating the new legislation, just as it fought for the original GI Bill [the Servicemen's Readjustment Act] more than 65 years ago. . . .

Between 1944 and 1956, millions of veterans took advantage of educational benefits provided by the original bill and helped to fill the nation's workforce with qualified and trained professionals. Although they no longer wore the military uniform, the veterans' contributions to the country weren't any less significant, he said. . . .

"This new Post-9/11 GI Bill has the potential to impact the country in the same way, thanks to your leadership and the leadership in this country," he added. "You've been our eyes and ears in identifying needs of veterans."

The education opportunities also will help VA in its struggle to end homelessness among veterans, which, Shinseki said, also will have an indirect but positive effect on a host of other issues.

Michael J. Carden,
"New GI Bill Will Heighten Professional Work Force,"
Defense.gov, American Forces Press Service, August 27, 2009.

To fill the key job of undersecretary for health, we've established a commission of senior executives from both public and private sectors, and we've tasked this commission with interviewing, evaluating, and recommending candidates for the post. Obviously we want someone who knows a lot about health care, but we also want someone who knows how to drive transformation within a large organization. The commission has narrowed the field now to just a handful of candidates, which the secretary will soon present to the White House, for the president to make the final selection.

Along with committed leadership, we need a trained and capable workforce dedicated to VA's principles: veteran-centric, results-oriented, and forward-looking. We need to re-orient the workforce we have toward the veterans themselves. We need to make advocacy—not just service, but advocacy on behalf of veterans and their dependents and survivors—our overriding philosophy. We also need to instill in our workers a greater level of personal accountability, while also creating a culture of openness and transparency so that workers aren't afraid to report problems.

That's our long-term leadership challenge—getting everyone thinking and acting the right way. In the short term, we have several close-in targets we can't ignore:

- We are scrambling to get 200,000 young veterans into college this fall [2009] under the Post-9/11 GI Bill [or the Post-9/11 Veterans Educational Assistance Act]. The first tuition checks will go out Monday [in August 2009]

- We are also working to expand services to 500,000 Priority 8 veterans who had lost their entitlements in 2003. We expect to add about half that number in the first year.

- We will be holding a mental health summit sometime before this year is out. Veterans lead the nation in joblessness, substance abuse, depression, homelessness, and suicides. 131,000 veterans sleep on our streets every night. Secretary Shinseki wants to take that down to zero in the next five years.

- We're also committed to reducing the backlog and processing times of disability claims so that veterans don't have to wait 6–12 months for their checks. The long-term solution here is business process redesign and information technology, but for now, we have the equivalent of the 82nd Airborne Division processing claims each and every day.

- IT [information technology] is also the solution to the problem of seamless transition from active duty to veteran status. In April, President Obama charged Secretary Shinseki and Defense Secretary [Robert] Gates with building a fully interoperable electronic records system that will provide each member of our armed forces with a virtual lifetime electronic record . . . to stay with them from the day they put on the uniform to the day they are laid to rest. With our leadership and experience, this new initiative will drive the improvement of health care through interoperable records, not just for veterans and service members, but also for the nation as a whole. It will also help speed up the claims process and eliminate delays in care and benefits.

From Adversary to Advocate

Further out, we're looking for new ways of thinking and acting. We are asking why 40 years after Agent Orange [a contaminated herbicide] was last used in Vietnam, this secretary is still adjudicating claims for service-connected disabilities related to it. And why 20 years after [Operation] Desert Storm, we are still debating the debilitating effects of whatever causes Gulf War illness. Left to our present processes, 20 or 40 years from now, some future secretary will be adjudicating service-connected disabilities from our ongoing conflicts, and veterans will still be seeing VA as their adversary instead of their advocate.

"With more female troops enlisting and returning home from combat every day, there is not a more urgent time to heed the words of [former president Abraham] Lincoln and care for she 'who has borne the battle.'"

The VA Is Ill-Prepared to Deal with the Growing Number of Female Veterans

Erin Mulhall

Erin Mulhall is the deputy policy director for research for the Iraq and Afghanistan Veterans of America (IAVA). In the following viewpoint, she elucidates the way in which female veterans have been underserved by the Department of Veterans Affairs (VA) and claims that one of the VA's biggest challenges is addressing the unique needs of female veterans. Mulhall argues that female veterans need easy, stable access to gender-specific care; better employment and housing support; and protection from harassment while on military duty.

Erin Mulhall, "Women Warriors: Supporting She 'Who Has Borne the Battle,'" Iraq and Afghanistan Veterans of America, October 2009. Reproduced by permission.

As you read, consider the following questions:

1. As IAVA asserts, what percentage of female veterans who use the VA suffer from at least one chronic medical condition?

2. According to the author, what is the key barrier that women face at the VA?

3. As of September 2009, how many homeless female veterans are there, according to the VA?

Women veterans face unique health care issues. Despite the fact that they are, on average, younger than male patients, 74 percent of women veterans who use the VA [Department of Veterans Affairs] suffer from at least one chronic medical condition. They are also more likely to have poor health status compared to male veterans who use the VA.

As a result of their service, women veterans also have different health care needs than their nonveteran peers. However, the health consequences for women deployed to a combat theater are still largely unknown, as no long-term studies on this topic have been completed. To address this knowledge gap, the VA currently has several studies under way regarding women veterans, their VA usage, and health concerns.

In addition, the VA is in the early stages of a longitudinal study of Iraq and Afghanistan veterans; the first results are tentatively due by 2012. The VA hopes to develop a better understanding of new veterans' issues, including the high rates of mental health injuries.

The High Rate of Mental Health Injuries

Although they are technically excluded from ground combat positions, many female troops have regularly seen combat while serving in Iraq and Afghanistan. As a result, female service members and veterans, like their male peers, are suffering from mental health injuries, such as post-traumatic stress disorder [PTSD] and major depression. According to a landmark 2008 study by the RAND Corporation, nearly 20 percent of Iraq and Afghanistan veterans, or about 300,000 people, report symptoms consistent with a diagnosis of post-traumatic stress disorder or depression.

Although in the general population, women develop PTSD as a result of traumatic experiences at more than twice the rate of men, it is not yet known whether female Iraq and Afghanistan veterans are experiencing higher rates of combat stress than their male peers. Some studies suggest that, historically, female service members are more prone to mental injuries than their male counterparts. However, the Army's Mental Health Advisory Team, which has been monitoring the morale and mental health of soldiers in Iraq since 2003, found that: "Female soldiers are no more vulnerable than male soldiers in how combat can affect their mental health and well-being."

The recent study by RAND offered the first look at the differences between genders in Iraq and Afghanistan veterans, finding that women were at a higher risk for reporting symptoms consistent with a diagnosis for PTSD and major depression. However, RAND researchers were not able to determine if other types of traumas or stressors aside from exposure to combat, such as military sexual trauma [MST], could have contributed to the increased risk. According to the VA, MST leads to a 59 percent higher risk for mental health injuries. Further study is needed to explore these initial findings.

Within the VA, female patients are more likely to have mental health issues than male patients, but that may be because female veterans are more likely to seek treatment for their psychological injuries than their male counterparts.

One of the biggest challenges facing the VA in the coming years is how to address the distinct health care needs of women veterans. Unfortunately, the VA is currently underprepared to meet this demand, and many female veterans are experiencing significant barriers to care.

Significant Barriers to Care

The VA acknowledges that women veterans have been chronically underserved. Despite the fact that they are more likely to have lower incomes and poor health, and less likely to have private health insurance, women veterans fulfill their health care needs outside of the VA more often than men do. The key barrier that women face at the VA is the fragmentation of women's services. Other barriers include lack of knowledge about eligibility and benefits, the perception that the VA is "unwelcoming" to women or does not provide adequate safety and privacy standards, and access to child care. These impediments will likely worsen, as the number of women veterans utilizing VA health care continues to grow.

The VA has taken some critical steps in recent years. As of June 2009, every VA hospital now has a full-time Women Veterans Program manager to coordinate services for women veterans. In addition, Dr. Michael Kussman, former VA undersecretary for health, instituted a work group in March 2008 to establish women's health at every facility according to the following guidelines: "That every women veteran has access to a VA primary care provider who can meet all her primary care needs, including gender-specific care, in the context of an ongoing patient-clinician relationship." However, despite its commitment, the VA has still not established a deadline for its facilities to meet the requirement of comprehensive primary care for women veterans, and some VA officials are even unclear on the steps needed to implement this new plan. Even with these measures, much more remains to be done to ensure that women veterans receive equitable, high-quality VA health care.

In 2003, the VA made it mandatory for all VA hospitals and clinics to provide a minimum level of women's health services, but only "where feasible." In addition, according to Dr. Patricia Hayes of the VA's Women Veterans Health Strategic Health Care Group, "the health care services delivered to women veterans have grown up in a patchwork fashion, with the delivery model based in part on the academic leanings of the women's health champion on site." As a result, the availability and quality of VA care for female veterans varies widely across the system.

On-site offering of gender-specific care has actually *declined* since 2003. Female veterans may be forced to travel more than two hours to receive routine gynecological care, such as a Pap smear or a breast exam. Where gender-specific care is available, it is often in multiple settings and performed by multiple providers, leading to fragmented care. For most women, this translates into having a primary care physician handle general health care while a second clinician may handle gender-specific needs, and in some cases, a third provider may address mental health issues. Unfortunately at the VA, comprehensive women's primary care clinics are "the exception rather than the rule." Only 14 percent of VA facilities offer specialized, comprehensive women's health clinics that serve as one-stop shops for primary care, gender-specific care, mental health services, and surgical services. In general, women's clinics typically operate half-time, and more than 40 percent offer only gender-specific exams.

A Shortage of Providers

In addition, women veterans often lack access to skilled providers in *women's health*, a term which encompasses gender-specific reproductive health care, care for health problems that are more common in women (like osteoporosis and depression), and care for health problems that affect women differently (like heart disease). According to the GAO [Government Accountability Office], the VA's ability to provide consistent and timely care to female veterans is being compromised by shortages of qualified women's health and mental health providers. Research shows that women veterans are significantly more satisfied with VA health care when they have

Types of Women's Health Clinics at VA Facilities

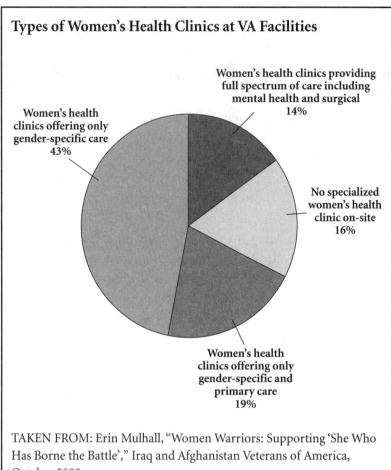

Women's health clinics offering only gender-specific care
43%

Women's health clinics providing full spectrum of care including mental health and surgical
14%

No specialized women's health clinic on-site
16%

Women's health clinics offering only gender-specific and primary care
19%

TAKEN FROM: Erin Mulhall, "Women Warriors: Supporting 'She Who Has Borne the Battle'," Iraq and Afghanistan Veterans of America, October 2009.

access to a women's health provider, especially if the provider is female and when the care can be provided by a gender-specific clinic.

Overall, women who had received treatment in women's health clinics were "more likely to rely solely on the VA for their health care, were more likely to have seen other VA providers, and were less likely to report using non-VA physicians." They also are more likely to report excellent satisfaction than those seen in traditional primary care clinics. Additional research should be undertaken to determine the optimum model of health care delivery for female veterans.

Another challenge that women veterans face is ensuring the continuity of their care across multiple health care systems. 51 percent of women VA users are splitting their care between the VA and an outside health care system. For many of these women, especially those in rural areas, there has been little evaluation of the overall quality of their care. Even less is known about the care that women veterans receive when they opt not to use the VA system.

While access to care is the primary obstacle for female veterans, they can also experience other barriers. The VA has traditionally been a passive system, and veterans must overcome tremendous bureaucratic hurdles to get the benefits and services that the VA provides. Female veterans, in particular, often do not know what they are eligible for.

Some women also perceive the VA as unwelcoming to them, as it relates to privacy and safety issues and quality of gender-specific services. In one VA study of female veterans who do not use the VA, researchers found that non-users described the VA as "dated Hollywood images of old soldiers in ward beds, antiquated facilities, and less qualified doctors." Other females have expressed concern about receiving care in the overly male-dominated VA environment.

In addition, despite its assurances, the VA is still not meeting privacy standards for women veterans at its facilities. In July 2009, the GAO found instances where women's exam room tables faced doors instead of walls, and where women patients had to walk through waiting rooms to use restrooms, as opposed to having them located next to exam rooms as required by VA policy. Some hospitals under review also did not guarantee access to private and secure bathing areas or visual and auditory privacy at check-in.

Underemployment and Homelessness

After they leave the military, women veterans have dramatically different employment experiences than men. On average, female veterans earn statistically more than their nonveteran peers, unlike their male counterparts.

According to the U.S. Census Bureau, this may be because "military education and work experience may translate into higher paying civilian jobs than women with a high school degree would normally expect." In addition, since women cannot hold ground combat jobs, their military skills may be more readily transferable to the civilian world than those of male veterans. In order to enjoy this earnings advantage, however, women veterans work longer hours and more weeks a year than women who have not served in the military. Additionally, female veterans on average earn almost $10,000 less a year than male veterans, and they often struggle to find jobs that pay what their military career did.

These lower incomes may be a factor in why women veterans are more likely to experience a severe housing cost burden than male veterans, placing them at significant risk for homelessness.

As of September 2009, the VA estimated that there are 13,100 homeless female veterans. Women veterans are up to four times more likely to be homeless than nonveteran women. Unfortunately, as more women join the armed forces, they are also swelling the ranks of the homeless. According to Pete Dougherty, director of homeless programs at the VA, "while the overall numbers [of homeless vets] have been going down, the number of women veterans who are homeless is going up."

Thousands of Iraq and Afghanistan veterans are joining over 100,000 veterans of other generations living on the streets and in shelters. Preliminary data from the VA suggest that Iraq and Afghanistan veterans make up 1.8 percent of the homeless veteran population. As of September 2009, more than 3,700 Iraq and Afghanistan veterans have already been seen in the Department of Veterans Affairs' homeless outreach program. Of homeless Iraq and Afghanistan veterans, more than 10 percent are women. Not all homeless Iraq and Afghanistan veterans use VA services however, so the real number of homeless Iraq and Afghanistan veterans may be considerably higher. In addition, because the homeless population is transient, and because many people may experience homelessness off and on over months or even years, correctly measuring the homeless population is difficult.

Female homeless veterans tend to have more severe mental health problems than homeless male veterans, in part because they are more likely to experience sexual trauma while serving in the military. The VA reports that about 40 percent of the homeless female veterans of recent wars say they were sexually assaulted by a fellow service member while in the military.

Not Enough Resources

But programs for homeless female veterans, and especially for those with children, have been "slow to materialize," according to the VA Advisory Committee on Homeless Veterans. Even the VA acknowledges that existing programs for women veterans are "probably not yet sufficient." With only about a dozen female-only facilities nationwide, women veterans often have to travel long distances or outside their state in order to have access to these options. Within the VA's homeless shelter system, only 60 percent of shelters can accept women, and less than 5 percent have programs that target female veterans specifically or offer separate housing from men.

Adding to the challenge is the increasing number of female veterans with families in need of homeless services; 23 percent of female veterans in the VA's homelessness programs have children under 18 years old. Since the VA cannot provide direct care to children or spouses of veterans, providing suitable housing for homeless veterans with families falls under the responsibility of multiple agencies, and coordinating this care can be extremely challenging. Homeless veterans have continually cited child care as their number one unmet need.

Throughout America's history, women have served honorably and sacrificed tremendously. And they continue this effort in Iraq and Afghanistan today. Yet, the nation is not doing enough to support them here at home.

Collectively, bold steps must be taken to improve health care for female troops and veterans—taking their unique health care needs into account—and expand existing support services and transitional resources. Female veterans should no longer have to choose between a homeless shelter and the streets at night. The military must also work aggressively to eliminate sexual assault and harassment from within its ranks, and widen career opportunities for women. This will make our military stronger and our country more secure. With more female troops enlisting and returning home from combat every day, there is not a more urgent time to heed the words of [former president Abraham] Lincoln and care for she "who has borne the battle." The brave women who answer our country's call deserve nothing less.

> "[The Department of Veterans Affairs] needs to keep pace with the changing needs of women who served in the military, and we are ready to take whatever steps are necessary in the future to properly assist women veterans."

The VA Is Working to Ensure That Needs of Female Veterans Are Met

Bradley G. Mayes

Bradley G. Mayes is the director of the Compensation and Pension Service at the Veterans Benefits Administration, U.S. Department of Veterans Affairs (VA). In the following viewpoint taken from his testimony before Congress, Mayes asserts that the VA recognizes the needs of the growing number of female veterans. Mayes reports that the VA is expanding existing programs as well as tailoring new ones for women's unique needs.

As you read, consider the following questions:

1. What is the VA's estimate of the number of female veterans?

Bradley G. Mayes, "Eliminating the Gaps: Examining Women Veterans' Issues," Statement Before the House Committee on Vetrans' Affairs, U.S. Department of Veterans Affairs, July 16, 2009.

2. The number of women receiving VA compensation and pension increased what percentage from 2006–2009?

3. According to Mayes, what can women veterans coordinators offer female veterans?

Although women have been associated with military activity since the founding of our nation, their role has increased dramatically in recent years. From the time of the American Revolution, women have supported the military service of their male counterparts and sometimes took up arms themselves. Their work and sacrifice as military nurses saved innumerable lives and contributed immeasurably to the efforts of all military campaigns. These medical efforts were especially valuable during World War II and the wars in Korea and Vietnam. However, despite their major contributions, the percentage of service members in these conflicts who were women was relatively small. According to U.S. Census Bureau statistics, 5 percent of veterans who served in World War II were women veterans, 2 percent who served in Korea were women veterans, and 3 percent who served in Vietnam were women veterans. However, during the Gulf War of 1991–1992, the percentage of women veterans increased to 16 percent. This reflects a significantly expanded role for women in the military. As a result, the Department of Veterans Affairs (VA) has adjusted its programs accordingly.

The expanded role of women in the military has also brought about increased responsibilities and risk taking. Women serving in Iraq and Afghanistan face combat activity similar to their male counterparts. As aircraft pilots, convoy transportation specialists, military police officers, and members of civilian pacification teams, women have increasingly been in harm's way and have incurred more service-related physical and mental disabilities as a result.

The following VA statistics illustrate the significance these changing roles have had on VA. America has approximately

1.8 million women veterans. They make up approximately 7.7 percent of the total number of veterans awarded service connection. The number of women receiving VA compensation and pension increased from 203,000 in 2006, to over 250,000 in June of 2009. This represents a 23 percent increase in less than 3 years. So far this fiscal year, the number of women veterans receiving benefits who served in the current overseas contingency operations has increased by nearly 10,000. Although women veterans represent 12 percent of those who served in these operations, they represent 15 percent of those awarded service connection for a disability.

VA Efforts to Assist Women Veterans

VA established the Advisory Committee on Women Veterans in 1983 as a panel of experts on issues and programs affecting women veterans. Since then, we have worked to implement its recommendations for improving services to women veterans. A major issue of current concern for this committee is the occurrence of military sexual trauma (MST) among women on active duty and the disabilities that may result. The committee has recommended that VA address this issue to the greatest extent possible.

The claims of women veterans who seek disability compensation for post-traumatic stress disorder (PTSD) based on MST are specifically addressed in VA's regulations at 38 CFR §3.304(f)(4). In 2002, VA amended its PTSD regulations to emphasize that, if a PTSD claim is based on in-service personal assault, which include MST claims, evidence from sources other than the veteran's military records may be used to corroborate the in-service traumatic event. Such evidence may include, but is not limited to, records from law enforcement authorities, rape crisis centers, mental health counseling centers, and hospitals, as well as statements from family members, associates, or clergy. Service medical and personnel records are also reviewed in order to discover evidence of be-

Women and the Military

- Women make up 15 percent of current active, [National] Guard and reserve forces.

- There are 1.8 million women among the 23.4 million living veterans.

- The number of women using the [services of the] VA [Department of Veterans Affairs] is expected to double in the next five years [from 2009].

- About one in five women who seek treatment from the VA report they experienced sexual trauma while in the military.

Rick Maze,
"Bills Aim to Improve Services for Female Vets,"
Army Times, April 7, 2009.

havior changes that may support the occurrence of the traumatic event. In addition, prior to a decision on the claim, VA provides an appropriate medical or mental health professional with the available evidence and asks for an opinion as to whether the traumatic event occurred. These procedures take into account the sensitive nature of MST and the difficulty in obtaining supporting evidence.

Unique Needs Must Be Met

Another general recommendation from the Advisory Committee on Women Veterans is that proper health care and compensation should be provided for service-connected disabilities that are unique to women veterans. Unique disability compensation evaluation criteria for women veterans are provided in the VA Schedule for Rating Disabilities under the section for gynecological conditions and disorders of the breast. An additional monetary benefit, referred to as special monthly compensation, is also available for loss, or loss of use, of a creative organ as the result of a service-connected disability. This applies to the male and female reproductive systems. In 2000, VA amended 38 CFR §3.350(a) to authorize special monthly compensation for women veterans who suffer a service-connected loss of 25 percent or more of breast tissue from a mastectomy or radiation treatment.

Congress has acknowledged the effects of herbicide exposure on women veterans who served in Vietnam and the potential for birth defects that may occur in their children as a result. Chapter 18 of title 38, United States Code, authorizes a monetary allowance for the children of any Vietnam veteran for disability attributable to spina bifida and for the children of women veterans who served in Vietnam for disability due to a covered birth defect. A long list of birth defects that qualify a child for a monetary allowance are described in VA regulations. This list reflects the findings of a VA study that indicated an association between numerous birth defects among the children of females, but not males, who were exposed to herbicides.

Outreach Efforts

As a further means to implement recommendations of the Advisory Committee on Women Veterans, the Veterans Benefits Administration (VBA) has engaged in outreach efforts. When active-duty military personnel are separated from service or National Guard and Reserve members are demobilized, VBA provides information to them under the Transition Assistance Program (TAP) at their military base. This pre-discharge program explains the array of benefits available from VA and assists individuals with filing disability claims. One mandatory section of TAP is a PowerPoint slide presentation on "military sexual and other personal trauma." This is intended to alert separating service members that VA is aware of the MST problem and inform them that counseling, treatment, and disability compensation are available.

Outreach efforts are also conducted at all VA regional offices on a continuing basis. Each regional office employs a women veterans coordinator who is well versed in personal trauma issues, including those of MST, as well as gender specific disability issues, and who acts as a liaison with the Women Veterans Program manager at the local VA health care facility. These coordinators also work with the regional office homeless veterans coordinators to address the problems of homeless women veterans. A nationwide VA women veterans coordinator training conference is scheduled for August 2009 in St. Paul, Minnesota. At the conference, VA will present updated information and skill training to the coordinators. Topics will include: outreach methods, clinical perspectives on personal trauma, and women veterans health issues. In addition to these personal outreach efforts, VBA maintains a public Internet Web site devoted to the unique issues associated with women veterans. This VBA Web site is in addition to Web sites maintained by the VA Center for Women Veterans and the Veterans Health Administration (VHA) on women veterans health care.

VA has recognized the service provided to our nation by women veterans and the importance of providing them with the assistance they deserve. VBA has moved forward, along with VHA, to address the issues that are unique to women veterans. We have developed special regulations for adjudication of PTSD claims based on MST. Regarding compensation for gender-specific disabilities, we provide special monthly compensation for breast tissue loss and monetary assistance for the children of women Vietnam veterans who develop birth defects. We have also engaged in nationwide outreach to facilitate women veterans' access to VA benefits. We realize that VA needs to keep pace with the changing needs of women who served in the military, and we are ready to take whatever steps are necessary in the future to properly assist women veterans.

| "Treatments that are effective in improving the health of veterans with Gulf War illness are urgently needed."

Not Enough Is Being Done for Veterans with Gulf War Illness

Research Advisory Committee on Gulf War Veterans' Illnesses

The Research Advisory Committee on Gulf War Veterans' Illnesses was appointed in 2002 to evaluate the effectiveness of government research in addressing the nature, causes, and treatments of Gulf War-related illnesses. In the following report, the organization notes that VA efforts to improve the health of Gulf War veterans suffering from Gulf War illness have largely failed. Therefore, the VA should act with urgency to commit expanded federal support to help veterans suffering with this affliction.

As you read, consider the following questions:

1. What percentage of the seven hundred thousand veterans who served in the Gulf War suffer from health problems, according to the viewpoint?

2. What symptoms constitute Gulf War illness, in the author's description?

Gulf War Illness and the Health of Gulf War Veterans: Scientific Findings and Recommendations. Boston: Research Advisory Committee on Gulf War Veterans' Illnesses, 2008.

3. Why does Gulf War illness pose a complex scientific challenge for researchers?

More than seventeen years have passed since the United States and its international allies liberated Kuwait from the grip of Saddam Hussein's Iraqi military forces in the 1990–1991 Gulf War. Despite the swift and decisive victory achieved in Operation Desert Storm, at least one-fourth of the nearly 700,000 U.S. military personnel who served in the war have experienced a complex of difficult and persistent health problems since their return home. Illness profiles typically include some combination of chronic headaches, cognitive difficulties, widespread pain, unexplained fatigue, chronic diarrhea, skin rashes, respiratory problems, and other abnormalities. This symptom complex, now commonly referred to as Gulf War illness, is not explained by routine medical evaluations or by psychiatric diagnoses, and has persisted, for many veterans, for 17 years. While specific symptoms can vary between individuals, a remarkably consistent illness profile has emerged from hundreds of reports and studies of different Gulf War veteran populations from different regions of the U.S., and from allied countries.

For many years, diverse views about the cause or causes of Gulf War illness have been put forward and vigorously debated. Hundreds of burning oil well fires that turned the Kuwaiti sky black with smoke, dramatic reports of uranium-tipped munitions, sandstorms, secret vaccines, and frequent chemical alarms, along with the government's acknowledgment of nerve agent releases in theater, led many to believe that veterans were suffering from effects of hazardous exposures that occurred during their deployment. Government officials and special committee reports maintained that there was little evidence that this was the case, and noted that veterans returning from other wars have often experienced chronic health problems related to the stressful circumstances of serving in a war zone. All sides called for research to better understand the problem. Multiple official investigations were launched and hundreds of research studies funded.

Studying the Issue of Gulf War Illness

In 1998, the U.S. Congress mandated the appointment of a public advisory panel of independent scientists and veterans to advise on federal research studies and programs to address the health consequences of the Gulf War. The Research Advisory Committee on Gulf War Veterans' Illnesses was appointed by the secretary of Veterans Affairs in 2002 and directed to evaluate the effectiveness of government research in addressing central questions on the nature, causes, and treatments of Gulf War-related illnesses. According to its charter, the guiding principle for the Committee's work is the premise that the fundamental goal of all Gulf War-related government research is to improve the health of Gulf War veterans, and the choice and success of federal Gulf War research should be judged accordingly.

The Committee has convened public meetings on a regular basis to consider the broad spectrum of scientific research, investigative reports, and government research activities related to the health of Gulf War veterans. In addition to annual reports on Committee meetings and activities, it has periodically issued formal scientific recommendations and reports. The Committee's last extended report, *Scientific Progress in Understanding Gulf War Veterans' Illnesses*, issued in 2004, provided findings and recommendations on topics the Committee had considered up to that time. The present report provides a comprehensive review of information and evidence on topics reviewed by the Committee since that time, as well as additional information on topics considered in the 2004 report.

The central focus of this report is Gulf War illness, the multisymptom condition that affects veterans of the 1990–1991 Gulf War at significantly elevated rates. Despite considerable government, scientific, and media attention, little was clearly understood about Gulf War illness for many years. Now, 17 years after the war, the extensive body of scientific research and government investigations that is currently available provides the basis for an evidence-based assessment of the nature and causes of Gulf War illness. As described throughout the report, scientific evidence leaves no question that Gulf War illness is a real condition with real causes and serious consequences for affected veterans. Research has also shown that this pattern of illness does not occur after every war and cannot be attributed to psychological stressors during the Gulf War.

Although Gulf War illness is the most prominent and widespread issue related to the health of Gulf War veterans, it is not the only one. Additional issues of importance include diagnosed medical and psychiatric conditions affecting Gulf War veterans, and questions related to the health of veterans' family members. . . .

Gulf War research has posed a complex scientific challenge for researchers. Most obviously, Gulf War illness does not fit neatly into well-established categories of disease. The underlying pathophysiology of Gulf War illness is not apparent from routine clinical tests, and the illness appears not to be the result of a single cause producing a well-known effect. There are relatively few sources of objectively measured data for studying Gulf War illness or its association with events and exposures in the Gulf War. Some observers have suggested that these complexities pose too difficult a challenge, and that it is unlikely that the nature and causes of Gulf War illness can ever be known. On the contrary, the Committee has found that the extensive scientific research and other diverse sources of information related to the health of Gulf War veterans paint a cohesive picture that yields important answers to basic questions about both the nature and causes of Gulf War ill-

Veterans Receiving Service-Connected Disability Benefits, End of Fiscal Year 2008

Period of Service	Number of Veterans	Estimated Total Annual Amounts Paid	Estimated Average Annual Amounts Paid
World War II	273,973	$2,627,612,238	$9,591
Korean Conflict	156,839	$1,571,234,485	$10,018
Vietnam Era	1,015,410	$13,757,989,123	$13,549
Gulf War	896,746	$7,218,392,201	$8,050
Peacetime Era	609,314	$5,098,924,866	$8,368
Total	**2,952,282**	**$30,274,152,913**	**$10,254**

TAKEN FROM: "Annual Benefits Report, Fiscal Year 2008," www.vba.va.gov, Veterans Benefits Administration, 2008, 16.

ness. These, in turn, provide direction for future research that is urgently needed to improve the health of Gulf War veterans. . . .

How Many Veterans Are Affected?

Gulf War illness is not the only health condition related to Gulf War service, but it is by far the most common. Gulf War illness prevalence estimates vary with the specific case definition used. Studies consistently indicate, however, that an excess of 25 to 32 percent of veterans who served in the 1990–1991 Gulf War are affected by a complex of multiple symptoms, variously defined, over and above rates in contemporary military personnel who did not deploy to the Gulf War. That means that between 175,000 and 210,000 of the nearly 700,000 U.S. veterans who served in the 1990–1991 Gulf War suffer from this persistent pattern of symptoms as a result of their wartime service.

Research has not supported early speculation that Gulf War illness is a stress-related condition. Large population-based studies of Gulf War veterans consistently indicate that

Gulf War illness is not the result of combat or other deployment stressors, and that rates of post-traumatic stress disorder (PTSD) and other psychiatric conditions are relatively low in Gulf War veterans. Gulf War illness differs fundamentally from trauma and stress-related syndromes that have been described after other wars. No Gulf War illness-type problem, that is, no widespread symptomatic illness not explained by medical or psychiatric diagnoses, has been reported in veterans who served in Bosnia in the 1990s or in current conflicts in Iraq and Afghanistan.

Epidemiologic studies indicate that rates of Gulf War illness vary in different subgroups of Gulf War veterans. Gulf War illness affects veterans who served in the Army and Marines at higher rates than those in the Navy and Air Force, and enlisted personnel more than officers. Studies also indicate that Gulf War illness rates differ according to where veterans were located during deployment, with highest rates among troops who served in forward areas. More specifically, studies consistently show that the rate of Gulf War illness is associated with particular exposures that veterans encountered during deployment.

Confusion Surrounds the Issue

Identified links between veteran-reported exposures and Gulf War illness have raised a great deal of interest, but have also been the source of considerable confusion. The use of self-reported exposure information raises a number of concerns, most obviously in relation to recall bias. These concerns emphasize the importance of assessing findings across a broad spectrum of studies, rather than relying on results from individual studies, and of evaluating the impact of recall and other information bias on study results where possible.

The Committee identified an additional problem that has had a profound effect on epidemiologic study results and their interpretation. Exposures assessed in Gulf War studies are highly correlated, that is, veterans who had one type of exposure also usually had many others. In analyzing the effects of any single exposure during the war, it is essential that effects of other exposures be considered and adjusted for, to avoid the well-known problem of "confounding," or confusing the effects of multiple exposures with one another. Many Gulf War epidemiologic studies failed to control for confounding effects, yielding illogical results that made it appear as if all, or nearly all, wartime exposures caused Gulf War illness. In contrast, adjusted results—that is, those that controlled for effects of other exposures in theater—consistently identified a very limited number of significant risk factors for Gulf War illness.

The Urgent Need for Effective Treatments

Gulf War illness has persisted for a very long time for most ill veterans—over seventeen years for many. Studies indicate that few veterans with Gulf War illness have recovered over time and only a small minority have substantially improved. The federal Gulf War research effort has yet to provide tangible results in achieving its ultimate objective, that is, to improve the health of Gulf War veterans. Few treatments have been studied and none have been shown to provide significant benefit for a substantial number of ill veterans.

Treatments that are effective in improving the health of veterans with Gulf War illness are urgently needed. In recent years, congressional actions have led to promising initiatives in this effort at both the Department of Defense (DoD) and the Department of Veterans Affairs (VA). At DoD, the Office of Congressionally Directed Medical Research Programs has developed an innovative program aimed at identifying treatments and diagnostic tests for Gulf War illness. The program funded a limited number of new treatment studies in 2007 and has invited proposals for additional studies to be funded in 2009. In addition, VA has sponsored a center of excellence for Gulf War research at the University of Texas Southwestern, focused on identifying specific biological abnormalities that underlie Gulf War illness that can be targeted for treatment. Research to identify effective treatments for Gulf War illness has been given highest priority by the Committee and requires expanded federal support.

> *"[The Department of Veterans Affairs] trains its providers to prepare to respond to the specific health care needs of all veterans, including Gulf War veterans with difficult-to-diagnose illnesses."*

The VA Offers a Wide Range of Programs for Veterans Suffering from Gulf War Illness

Lawrence Deyton

Lawrence Deyton is the chief public health and environmental hazards officer in the Veterans Health Administration. In the following viewpoint taken from his testimony given before Congress, Deyton acknowledges that Gulf War veterans are suffering from a range of health problems as a result of their service overseas. Deyton outlines the research and initiatives the Department of Veterans Affairs (VA) has implemented in order to help veterans suffering from Gulf War illness.

Lawrence Deyton, "Gulf War Illness Research: Is Enough Being Done?" Statement Before Committee on Veterans' Affairs, House Committee on Veterans' Affairs, May 19, 2009.

As you read, consider the following questions:

1. What three questions does the VA's research focus on, according to Deyton?

2. What were the findings of the VA's clinical registry examination?

3. Name an initiative taken by the VA that is tailored for Gulf War veterans.

VA [Department of Veterans Affairs] recognizes that veterans returning from combat often face unique medical conditions; indeed, providing health care for these conditions is part of our core mission. Research supported directly or indirectly by VA has identified a number of health problems for which deployed veterans face greater risks. In response to these findings, VA has adapted its health care system to provide support, treatment and counseling for affected veterans and their dependents. . . .

The United States deployed nearly 700,000 military personnel to the Kuwaiti Theater of Operations (KTO) during Operations Desert Shield and Desert Storm (August 2, 1990, through July 31, 1991). Within months of their return, some Gulf War veterans reported various symptoms and illnesses they believed were related to their service. Veterans, their families, and VA subsequently became concerned about the possible adverse health effects from various environmental exposures during Operations Desert Shield and Desert Storm.

Of particular concern have been the symptoms and illnesses that, to date, have eluded specific diagnosis. To date, 111,000 Gulf War veterans have enrolled in VA's health registry, and approximately 59,000 have enrolled in the Department of Defense's (DoD's) registry. In addition, more than 335,000 have been seen at least once as patients by VA. Although the majority of veterans seeking VA health care had readily diagnosable health conditions, we remain very concerned about veterans whose symptoms could not be diagnosed. VA continues to compensate and treat these conditions, even without a clear diagnosis.

Gulf War Illness Research

VA's Office of Research and Development (ORD) recognized soon after veterans began returning from the 1991 Gulf War that while there were few visible casualties, many individuals returned from this conflict with unexplained medical symptoms and illnesses. ORD supports a research portfolio consisting of studies dedicated to understanding chronic multi-symptom illnesses, long-term health effects of potentially hazardous substances to which Gulf War veterans may have been exposed during deployment, and conditions or symptoms that may be occurring with higher prevalence in Gulf War veterans, such as amyotrophic lateral sclerosis (ALS), multiple sclerosis [MS] and brain cancer. VA's research focus in this area considers three principal questions:

- First, what, if any, conditions do Gulf War veterans report at a disproportionate rate to the civilian population or to non-deployed veterans?

- Second, what are the causes of these conditions?

- Third, what is the best approach for treating these conditions?

These research agendas are supported and complemented by the work of a range of partners, both inside government and out. For example, the VA/DoD Health Executive Council oversees the research subcommittee of the Deployment Health Work Group, and the Department of Health and Human Services [HHS] participates in both the Deployment Health Work Group and its research subcommittee. This cooperation provides essential data on military and civilian populations and reflects some of the best research from across the country. Some exposures service members face while deployed in combat are actually quite similar to domestic exposures, so inclusion of civilian studies provides an important perspective on what risks exist under different situations or at different levels of exposure. For example, pesticides are commonly used by citizens every day, and these same pesticides are also often used in military theaters of combat. Moreover, data from DoD have proven essential to VA's epidemiological studies of the veteran cohort. Specifically, following the end of active hostilities in the Gulf War, DoD provided VA with data on approximately 690,000 returning veterans. This data establishes a broad research base that improves its validity and reliability concerning health risks for veterans. This research is not purely academic; policy makers use these findings to make health care decisions regarding resources, treatment and presumptive connections to military service.

The VA's Health Examination Registry

Following the end of active combat in the Gulf War, VA quickly established a clinical registry to screen for health problems attributable to intense smoke from oil fires. The voluntary health registry examination also encouraged new combat veterans to take advantage of VA health care programs. VA has long maintained health registries on other at-risk populations, including veterans exposed to ionizing radiation and Vietnam veterans exposed to Agent Orange [a contaminated herbicide]. Formally established by law in 1992, VA's Gulf War veterans' health examination registry is still available to all Gulf War veterans, including veterans of the current conflict in Iraq. It offers a comprehensive physical examination and collects data from participating veterans about their symptoms, diagnoses, and self-reported Gulf War hazardous exposures.

As of March 2009, this program evaluated over 110,000 Gulf War veterans, or about one in seven veterans. The program has also seen nearly 7,000 veterans who served in the current conflict in Iraq, who as Gulf War veterans themselves are eligible for this program.

After 15 years, the principal finding from VA's systematic clinical registry examination of about 16 percent of 1991 Gulf War veterans is that they are suffering from a wide variety of common and recognized illnesses. However, no new or unique syndrome has been identified. VA recognizes that registry data has significant limitations. Registry participants are self-selected and do not necessarily represent all veterans. Additionally, any findings from a registry are limited to that population and do not demonstrate whether veterans are receiving any diagnoses at rates different than expected. High-quality epidemiological research studies are the best approach for evaluating the health impacts of service in the 1991 Gulf War (or in any deployment). These studies are greatly facilitated by VA's electronic medical record, which summarizes every visit by a veteran and includes all medical diagnoses.

Investigating Environmental Factors

VA also works closely with the National Academy of Sciences' (NAS) Institute of Medicine (IOM) to evaluate potential associations between environmental hazards encountered during military deployment and specific health effects. Since 1991, IOM has completed nineteen independent reviews of Gulf War veterans' health issues. VA has pursued this relationship with IOM at its own discretion and upon recommendation by Congress for Vietnam and Gulf War veterans, as well as veterans of other eras such as today's conflicts in Iraq and Afghanistan. IOM's work has allowed VA to recognize approximately a dozen diseases as presumed to be connected to exposure to Agent Orange and other herbicides used during the Vietnam War, and to the dioxin impurity some contained. IOM's opinion is regularly sought to address a range of health care issues. Their independent stature and collection of internationally recognized scholars and researchers uniquely positions the IOM to provide expert, well-informed findings free of conflicts of interest. When VA works with IOM, we generally defer to their professional opinions concerning methodology to support this independence. Their reports consider all available research, including both human and animal studies, to guide their findings about whether there is a connection between exposure to a substance or hazard and the occurrence of an illness and whether there is a plausible biological mechanism or other evidence to support that connection. IOM bases their recommendations upon formal findings and scientific evidence, and each IOM report is reviewed internally and externally in an exacting and thorough process.

In 1998, in response to increasing health concerns among veterans of the 1991 Gulf War, Congress enacted Public Law 105-368 requiring VA and DoD to seek to contract with the National Academy of Sciences under which IOM would provide an independent analysis of the published peer-reviewed literature on possible long-term health effects from environmental and occupational hazards associated with the 1991 Gulf War. This process has generated nine comprehensive IOM committee reports on a wide variety of Gulf War health issues including long-term health effects from vaccines, depleted uranium, nerve agent antidotes, chemical warfare agents, pesticides, solvents, fuels, oil well smoke, infectious diseases, deployment-related stress, traumatic brain injury, and Gulf War veteran epidemiological studies.

Establishing the RACGWVI

At the direction of Congress, VA, in 2002 chartered the VA Research Advisory Committee on Gulf War Veterans' Illnesses (RACGWVI) to advise the secretary on the overall effectiveness of federally funded research to answer central questions on the nature, causes, and treatments of Gulf War–associated illnesses. The RACGWVI's charter stipulates that they are to

Gulf War Illness Symptoms by Country

	United States	United Kingdom	Canada	Australia
Skin condition	20–21%	21%	4–7%	4%
Arthritis/joint problem	6–11%	10%	−1–3%	2%
Gastrointestinal problems	15%	—	5–7%	1%
Respiratory problem	4–7%	2%	2–5%	1%
Chronic Fatigue Syndrome	1–4%	3%	—	0%
Post-Traumatic Stress Disorder	3–6%	9%	6%	3%
Chronic Mental Illness	13–25%	26%	—	—

TAKEN FROM: Barbara LaClair, Research Advisory Committee on Gulf War Veterans' Illnesses Meeting Minutes: Appendix A, Presentation 1, December 12–13, 2005, 71.

provide information to the VA and not to independently release information. Despite their charter restrictions, the RACGWVI has published and released an independent report, including recommendations, in 2004 and again in 2008. The 2008 RACGWVI report and recommendations from the RACGWVI were presented to the former secretary in November 2008.

In November 2008, VA requested that the IOM explain discrepancies between findings contained in nine congressionally mandated IOM committee reports on Gulf War health issues completed since 1998, and the October 2008 report released by the RACGWVI. On January 23, 2009, VA received a response from Dr. Harvey Fineberg, president of the IOM.

- In summary, these nine independent IOM committee reports have found that Gulf War veterans experience greater rates of symptom-based illnesses compared to their non-deployed peers, but no unique illness has been identified. Further, most of the environmental hazards reviewed have not been found to explain illnesses experienced by Gulf War veterans.

- In contrast, the October 2008 RACGWVI report concluded that a unique neurological illness has caused significant morbidity (25 percent) among Gulf War veterans, and that this is "causally" (the highest possible level of association) linked to nerve agent antidote pyridostigmine bromide and pesticides used in the 1991 Gulf War. . . .

VA Provides Reports on Progress

VA has traditionally and by law relied upon the IOM for independent and credible reviews of the science behind these particular veterans' health issues, therefore, VA will consider the IOM review of the advisory committee's report before the department officially responds to its conclusions.

VA prepares an annual report to Congress that describes federally sponsored research on Gulf War veterans' illnesses and has done so every year since 1997. In the 2007 report, VA provided updated information on 19 research topics in five major research areas and a complete project listing by research focus area. The research areas include: brain and nervous system function, environmental toxicology, immune function, reproductive health, and symptoms and general health status. The 2007 report noted that between fiscal year (FY) 1992 and FY 2007, VA, DoD, and HHS funded 345 distinct projects related to health problems affecting Gulf War veterans. Funding for this research on the health care needs of Gulf War veterans has totaled nearly $350 million over this period of time. These projects varied from small pilot studies to large-scale epidemiological surveys. Nine projects were funded through the Gulf War Veterans' Illnesses research program and three were funded through the Peer Reviewed Medical Research Program. Both programs are managed by the Congressionally Directed Medical Research Programs at DoD. VA funded two new projects in FY 2007, with one focused on environmental toxicology and the other on symptoms and general health.

Treatment and Care

Research is only the first step of the process; by turning information into action, VA directly improves the care of veterans. As noted before, veterans face both common and unique health care concerns when compared with the private sector, and VA physicians are prepared to deal with both. VA trains its providers to prepare to respond to the specific health care needs of all veterans, including Gulf War veterans with difficult-to-diagnose illnesses. For Gulf War veterans, VA developed a clinical practice guideline on post-combat deployment health and another dealing with diagnosis of unexplained pain and fatigue. Also, VA has established three War Related Illness and Injury Study Centers to provide specialized health care for combat veterans from all deployments who experience difficult to diagnose or undiagnosed but disabling illnesses. Based on lessons learned from the Gulf War, VA anticipates concerns about unexplained illness after virtually all deployments, including Operation Enduring Freedom [in Afghanistan] and Operation Iraqi Freedom (OEF/OIF), and we are building our understanding of such illnesses.

This approach now includes OEF/OIF veterans with mild to moderate traumatic brain injury (TBI). VA's third War Related Illness and Injury Study Center at the VA Palo Alto Health Care System utilizes the advantages of the Polytrauma Rehabilitation Center, interdisciplinary program on blast injuries, and other specialty areas. VA has found combat injuries among OEF/OIF veterans are more likely to involve some degree of TBI than veterans of previous combat eras, and many of the long-term chronic health effects of TBI appear similarly difficult to diagnose.

Veterans Health Initiative Independent Study Guides

Following the Gulf War, VA developed the Veterans Health Initiative independent study guides for health care providers as one of many options to provide tailored care and support of veterans. This study guide was principally designed for veterans of that era, but has proven highly relevant for treating OEF/OIF veterans since many of the hazardous deployment-related exposures have proven to be the same. VA developed other independent study guides for returning veterans from Iraq and Afghanistan that cover topics such as gender and health care; infectious diseases of southwest Asia; military sexual trauma; and health effects from chemical, biological and radiological weapons. Study guides on post-traumatic stress disorder and TBI were also developed and made available for primary care physicians to increase understanding and awareness of these conditions. It is important to remember that the Veterans Health Initiative study guides are only one resource for providers. Dedicated staff members in VA medical centers are available to discuss any concerns veterans or providers may have regarding exposures they experienced while in a combat theater. VA distributes similar information through newsletters, brochures, conference calls and study centers to sensitize providers to the unique needs of combat veterans.

VA operates a range of programs that offer additional services and benefits to veterans and their dependents because of evidence that suggests a connection between military service and a health care deficit. For example, VA extends benefits to children of Vietnam veterans born with spina bifida as a presumed service-connected condition. Spina bifida is a devastating birth defect resulting from the failure of the spine to close. Depending on the extent of spinal damage, problems resulting from spina bifida may include permanent paralysis, orthopedic deformities, cognitive disabilities, breathing problems or impaired basic bodily functions. Likewise, the Children of Women Vietnam Veterans program provides hospital care and medical services for children with specific birth defects related to their veteran parent's military service. A monetary allowance is payable under both programs based on the child's degree of permanent disability.

VA Challenges

VA is an evolving organization that operates in a rapidly changing environment. Veterans from a broad background with unique needs come to us for care, and their military service sometimes exposes them to substances that may not be common in the civilian community and that may have unknown health effects. We have established a wide variety of programs to address these health concerns. At the same time, VA continues to learn new lessons to provide better care to all veterans, past, present, and future.

Periodical Bibliography

The following articles have been selected to supplement the diverse views presented in this chapter.

Bryan Bender	"More Female Veterans Are Winding Up Homeless," *Boston Globe*, July 6, 2009.
Michelle Chen	"Home from the Military," *ColorLines*, July–August 2008. www.colorlines.com.
Joseph R. Chenelly	"Helping Gulf War Veterans," *DAV Magazine*, March–April 2010.
Jia-Rui Chong	"Gulf War Syndrome Revisited," *Los Angeles Times*, March 11, 2008.
Beth Hawkins	"Another Gulf War Syndrome?" *Mother Jones*, March–April 2010.
Kimberly Hefling	"Female Veterans Struggle for Acceptance," *Huffington Post*, December 14, 2009.
Kimberly Hefling	"VA to Reopen Gulf War Vets' Files," Associated Press, February 26, 2010.
Jane Salodof MacNeil	"For Many Female Vets, PTSD Tied to Sex Trauma," *Clinical Psychiatry News*, December 1, 2006.
Amanda Ruggeri	"Female Veterans Fight for Healthcare," *U.S. News & World Report*, July 31, 2009.
Thom Wilborn	"VA Seeks to End Veterans Homelessness," *DAV Magazine*, January–February 2010.

OPPOSING
VIEWPOINTS®
SERIES

CHAPTER 3

How Does the VA Address Emerging and Controversial Health Issues?

Chapter Preface

In recent years, traumatic brain injury (TBI, also known as intracranial injury) has emerged as a growing threat to combat soldiers, with the consequences affecting thousands of U.S. military veterans of the Iraq and Afghanistan wars. TBI occurs when the brain is traumatically injured by an outside force such as the blast from a nearby improvised explosive device (IED). After the blast, the brain trauma causes secondary injury, which may include increased pressure within the skull and alterations in cerebral blood flow that may result in substantial additional injury to the brain.

A veteran suffering from TBI can experience a range of physical, cognitive, emotional, and behavioral effects. Research has found that 5–15 percent of mild TBI cases result in problems such as loss of short-term memory, decreased problem-solving skills, blurred vision, irritability, sleep disorders, and severe headaches. However, depending on the type and severity of the injury, some veterans suffering from TBI can make a full recovery. Others suffer from permanent disability or die from the injury. Treatment may include surgery, medication, physical and cognitive rehabilitation, and behavioral therapy.

A study conducted by the RAND Corporation in 2008 estimated that three hundred thousand U.S. troops may have suffered from TBI, most from blast-induced injuries. Since 2003, approximately one hundred thousand soldiers have been diagnosed with mild cases of TBI. With screening technologies becoming more advanced and comprehensive, experts believe that the number of cases of TBI among veterans will increase dramatically.

The Department of Veterans Affairs (VA) and the Department of Defense (DoD) have struggled to provide services for the increasing number of veterans diagnosed with TBI. Because the symptoms vary with each individual, the treatment must be tailored to each patient. Much of the struggle for the VA has to do with outreach—educating veterans as to the symptoms and treatment as well as providing screenings to identify injuries of this kind. Once a diagnosis is determined, a behavioral team can evaluate the test results to plan a course of treatment for the patient.

TBI is a devastating problem for Iraq and Afghanistan veterans—one the U.S. government is struggling to address with a range of effective programs. The debate on whether the VA is doing an adequate job helping veterans with TBI is just one of the topics included in this chapter. Another emerging health issue considered is the controversy over post-traumatic stress disorder (PTSD) diagnoses and whether the VA is deliberately misdiagnosing patients to save money. On the other hand, some argue that PTSD is being over-diagnosed among U.S. military veterans. The final controversy discussed in this chapter examines the VA's treatment of Gulf War illness.

> *"Interviews with soldiers diagnosed with personality disorder suggest that the military is using the psychological condition as a catch-all diagnosis, encompassing symptoms as diverse as deafness, headaches and schizophrenic delusions."*

The VA Is Misdiagnosing Veterans in Order to Deny Benefits

Joshua Kors

Joshua Kors is a reporter who writes frequently for the Nation. *In the following viewpoint, he investigates the charges that doctors from the Department of Veterans Affairs (VA) have been misdiagnosing soldiers wounded in Iraq with personality disorders instead of post-traumatic stress disorder (PTSD) to deny them VA benefits. Kors claims the VA is saving billions of dollars in expenses through this practice. But in some cases, doctors are intentionally deceiving soldiers, he asserts, and those veterans with misdiagnoses and their families suffer long-term financial and health costs.*

As you read, consider the following questions:

1. What happens if a soldier has not served his full contract before "Separation Because of Personality Disorder"?

2. According to the Defense Department, how many U.S. soldiers, across the entire armed forces, were dismissed due to personality disorders from 2001–2007?

3. According to army regulations, what conditions must be met for a personality disorder diagnosis?

Jon Town has spent the last few years fighting two battles, one against his body, the other against the U.S. Army. Both began in October 2004 in Ramadi, Iraq. He was standing in the doorway of his battalion's headquarters when a 107-millimeter rocket struck two feet above his head. The impact punched a piano-sized hole in the concrete facade, sparked a huge fireball and tossed the 25-year-old army specialist to the floor, where he lay blacked out among the rubble.

"The next thing I remember is waking up on the ground." Men from his unit had gathered around his body and were screaming his name. "They started shaking me. But I was numb all over," he says. "And it's weird because . . . because for a few minutes you feel like you're not really there. I could see them, but I couldn't hear them. I couldn't hear anything. I started shaking because I thought I was dead."

Eventually the rocket shrapnel was removed from Town's neck and his ears stopped leaking blood. But his hearing never really recovered, and in many ways, neither has his life. A soldier honored twelve times during his seven years in uniform, Town has spent the last three struggling with deafness, memory failure and depression. By September 2006 he and the army agreed he was no longer combat-ready.

But instead of sending Town to a medical board and discharging him because of his injuries, doctors at Fort Carson,

Colorado, did something strange: They claimed Town's wounds were actually caused by a "personality disorder." Town was then booted from the army and told that under a personality disorder discharge, he would never receive disability or medical benefits.

Town is not alone. A six-month investigation has uncovered multiple cases in which soldiers wounded in Iraq are suspiciously diagnosed as having a personality disorder, then prevented from collecting benefits. The conditions of their discharge have infuriated many in the military community, including the injured soldiers and their families, veterans' rights groups, even military officials required to process these dismissals.

They say the military is purposely misdiagnosing soldiers like Town and that it's doing so for one reason: to cheat them out of a lifetime of disability and medical benefits, thereby saving billions in expenses.

The Fine Print

In the army's separations manual it's called Regulation 635-200, Chapter 5-13: "Separation Because of Personality Disorder." It's an alluring choice for a cash-strapped military because enacting it is quick and cheap. The Department of Veterans Affairs [VA] doesn't have to provide medical care to soldiers dismissed with personality disorder. That's because under Chapter 5-13, personality disorder is a preexisting condition. The VA is only required to treat wounds sustained during service.

Soldiers discharged under 5-13 can't collect disability pay either. To receive those benefits, a soldier must be evaluated by a medical board, which must confirm that he is wounded and that his wounds stem from combat. The process takes several months, in contrast with a 5-13 discharge, which can be wrapped up in a few days.

If a soldier dismissed under 5-13 hasn't served out his contract, he has to give back a slice of his re-enlistment bonus as well. That amount is often larger than the soldier's final paycheck. As a result, on the day of their discharge, many injured vets learn that they owe the army several thousand dollars.

Spreading Misinformation

One military official says doctors at his base are doing more than withholding this information from wounded soldiers; they're actually telling them the opposite: that if they go along with a 5-13, they'll get to keep their bonus and receive disability and medical benefits. The official, who demanded anonymity, handles discharge papers at a prominent army facility. He says the soldiers he works with know they don't have a personality disorder. "But the doctors are telling them, this will get you out quicker, and the VA will take care of you. To stay out of Iraq, a soldier will take that in a heartbeat. What they don't realize is, those things are lies. The soldiers, they don't read the fine print," he says. "They don't know to ask for a med board. They're taking the word of the doctors. Then they sit down with me and find out what a 5-13 really means—they're shocked."

Russell Terry, founder of the Iraq War Veterans Organization (IWVO), says he's watched this scenario play itself out many times. For more than a year, his veterans' rights group has been receiving calls from distraught soldiers discharged under Chapter 5-13. Most, he says, say their military doctors pushed the personality disorder diagnosis, strained to prove that their problems existed before their service in Iraq and refused to acknowledge evidence of post-traumatic stress disorder (PTSD), traumatic brain injury and physical traumas, which would allow them to collect disability and medical benefits.

"These soldiers are coming home from Iraq with all kinds of problems," Terry says. "They go to the VA for treatment, and they're turned away. They're told, 'No, you have a preexisting condition, something from childhood.'" That leap in logic boils Terry's blood. "Everybody receives a psychological screening when they join the military. What I want to know is, if all these soldiers really did have a severe preexisting condition, how did they get into the military in the first place?"

Terry says that trying to reverse a 5-13 discharge is a frustrating process. A soldier has to claw through a thicket of paperwork, appeals panels and backstage political dealing, and even with the guidance of an experienced advocate, few are successful. "The 5-13," he says, "it's like a scarlet letter you can't get taken off."

A Growing Trend

In the last six years [2001–2006] the army has diagnosed and discharged more than 5,600 soldiers because of personality disorder, according to the Defense Department. And the numbers keep rising: 805 cases in 2001, 980 cases in 2003, 1,086 from January to November 2006. "It's getting worse and worse every day," says the official who handles discharge papers. "At my office the numbers started out normal. Now it's up to three or four soldiers each day. It's like, suddenly everybody has a personality disorder."

The reason is simple, he says. "They're saving a buck. And they're saving the VA money too. It's all about money."

Exactly how much money is difficult to calculate. Defense Department records show that across the entire armed forces, more than 22,500 soldiers have been dismissed due to personality disorders in the last six years. How much those soldiers would have collected in disability pay would have been determined by a medical board, which evaluates just how disabled a veteran is. A completely disabled soldier receives about $44,000 a year. In a recent study on the cost of veterans ben-

Perceived Barriers to Seeking Mental Health Services among Soldiers and Marines

Respondents were asked to rate "each of the possible concerns that might affect your decision to receive mental health counseling or services if you ever had a problem." The five possible responses ranged from "strongly disagree" to "strongly agree," with "agree" and "strongly agree" combined as a positive response.

Perceived Barrier	Respondents Who Met Screening Criteria for a Mental Disorder (N=731)	Respondents Who Did Not Meet Screening Criteria for a Mental Disorder (N=5422)
	no./total no. (%)	
I don't trust mental health professionals.	241/641 (38)	813/4820 (17)
I don't know where to get help.	143/639 (22)	303/4780 (6)
I don't have adequate transportation.	117/638 (18)	279/4770 (6)
It is difficult to schedule an appointment.	288/638 (45)	789/4748 (17)
There would be difficulty getting time off work for treatment.	354/643 (55)	1061/4743 (22)
Mental health care costs too much money.	159/638 (25)	456/4736 (10)
It would be too embarrassing.	260/641 (41)	852/4752 (18)
It would harm my career.	319/640 (50)	1134/4738 (24)
Members of my unit might have less confidence in me.	377/642 (59)	1472/4763 (31)
My unit leadership might treat me differently.	403/637 (63)	1562/4744 (33)
My leaders would blame me for the problem.	328/642 (51)	928/4769 (20)
I would be seen as weak.	413/640 (65)	1486/4732 (31)
Mental health care doesn't work.	158/638 (25)	444/4748 (9)

TAKEN FROM: Charles Hoge, et al, "Combat Duty in Iraq and Afghanistan, Mental Health Problems, and Barriers to Care," *New England Journal of Medicine*, July 1, 2004.

efits for the Iraq and Afghanistan wars, Harvard professor Linda Bilmes estimates an average disability payout of $8,890 per year and a future life expectancy of forty years for soldiers returning from service.

Using those figures, by discharging soldiers under Chapter 5-13, the military could be saving upwards of $8 billion in disability pay. Add to that savings the cost of medical care over the soldiers' lifetimes. Bilmes estimates that each year the VA spends an average of $5,000 in medical care per veteran. Applying those numbers, by discharging 22,500 soldiers because of personality disorders, the military saves $4.5 billion in medical care over their lifetimes.

A Broken Promise?

Town says Fort Carson psychologist Mark Wexler assured him that he would receive disability benefits, VA medical care and that he'd get to keep his bonus—good news he discussed with Christian Fields and Brandon Murray, two soldiers in his unit at Fort Carson. "We talked about it many times," Murray says. "Jon said the doctor there promised him benefits, and he was happy about it. Who wouldn't be?" Town shared that excitement with his wife, Kristy, shortly after his appointment with Wexler. "He said that Wexler had explained to him that he'd get to keep his benefits," Kristy says, "that the doctor had looked into it, and it was all coming with the chapter he was getting."

In fact, Town would not get disability pay or receive long-term VA medical care. And he would have to give back the bulk of his $15,000 bonus. Returning that money meant Town would leave Fort Carson less than empty-handed: He now owed the army more than $3,000. "We had this on our heads the whole way, driving home to Ohio," says Town. Wexler made him promises, he says, about what would happen if he went along with the diagnosis. "The final day, we find out, none of it was true. It was a total shock. I felt like I'd been betrayed by the army."

Wexler denies discussing benefits with Town. In a statement, the psychologist writes, "I have never discussed benefits with my patients as that is not my area of expertise. The only thing I said to Spc. [Specialist] Town was that the Chapter 5-13 is an honorable discharge. . . . I assure you, after over 15 years in my position, both as active duty and now civilian, I don't presume to know all the details about benefits and therefore do not discuss them with my patients."

Wexler's boss, Col. [Colonel] Steven Knorr, chief of the Department of Behavioral Health at Evans U.S. Army Hospital, declined to speak about Town's case. When asked if doctors at Fort Carson were assuring patients set for a 5-13 discharge that they'll receive disability benefits and keep their bonuses, Knorr said, "I don't believe they're doing that."

Not the Man He Used to Be

Interviews with soldiers diagnosed with personality disorder suggest that the military is using the psychological condition as a catch-all diagnosis, encompassing symptoms as diverse as deafness, headaches and schizophrenic delusions. That flies in the face of the army's own regulations.

According to those regulations, to be classified a personality disorder, a soldier's symptoms had to exist before he joined the military. And they have to match the "personality disorder" described in the *Diagnostic and Statistical Manual of Mental Disorders*, the national standard for psychiatric diagnosis. Town's case provides a clear window into how these personality disorder diagnoses are being used because even a cursory examination of his case casts grave doubt as to whether he fits either criterion.

Town's wife, for one, laughs in disbelief at the idea that her husband was suffering from hearing loss before he headed to Iraq. But since returning, she says, he can't watch TV unless the volume is full-blast, can't use the phone unless its volume is set to high. Medical papers from Fort Carson list Town as having no health problems before serving in Iraq; after, a Fort Carson audiologist documents "functional (non-organic) hearing loss." Town says his right ear, his "good" ear, has lost 50 percent of its hearing; his left is still essentially useless.

He is more disturbed by how his memory has eroded. Since the rocket blast, he has struggled to retain new information. "Like, I'll be driving places, and then I totally forget where I'm going," he says. "Numbers, names, dates—unless I knew them before, I pretty much don't remember." When Town returned to his desk job at Fort Carson, he found himself straining to recall the army's regulations. "People were like, 'What are you, dumb?' And I'm like, 'No, I'm probably smarter than you. I just can't remember stuff,'" he says, his melancholy suddenly replaced by anger. "They don't understand—I got hit by a rocket."

Those bursts of rage mark the biggest change, says Kristy Town. She says the man she married four years ago was "a real goofball. He'd do funny voices and faces—a great Jim Carrey imitation. When the kids would get a boo-boo, he'd fall on the ground and pretend he got a boo-boo too." Now, she says, "his emotions are all over the place. He'll get so angry at things, and it's not toward anybody. It's toward himself. He blames himself for everything." He has a hard time sleeping and doesn't spend as much time as he used to with the kids. "They get rowdy when they play, and he just has to be alone. It's almost like his nerves can't handle it."

Kristy begins to cry, pauses, before forcing herself to continue. She's been watching him when he's alone, she says. "He kind of . . . zones out, almost like he's in a daze."

More Problems for Specialist Town

In May 2006 Town tried to electrocute himself, dropping his wife's hair dryer into the bathtub. The dryer short-circuited before it could electrify the water. Fort Carson officials put Town in an off-post hospital that specializes in suicidal depression. Town had been promoted to corporal after returning from Iraq; he was stripped of that rank and reduced back to specialist. "When he came back, I tried to be the same," Kristy says. "He just can't. He's definitely not the man he used to be."

Town says his dreams have changed too. They keep taking him back to Ramadi, to the death of a good friend who'd been too near an explosion, taken too much shrapnel to the face. In his dreams Town returns there night after night to soak up the blood.

He stops his description for a rare moment of levity. "Sleep didn't used to be like that," he says. "I used to sleep just fine."

How the army determined then that Town's behavioral problems existed before his military service is unclear. Wexler, the Fort Carson psychologist who made the diagnosis, didn't interview any of Town's family or friends. It's unclear whether he even questioned Town's fellow soldiers in 2-17 Field Artillery, men like Fields, Murray and Michael Forbus, who could have testified to his stability and award-winning performance before the October 2004 rocket attack. As Forbus puts it, before the attack Town was "one of the best in our unit"; after, "the son of a gun was deaf in one ear. He seemed lost and disoriented. It just took the life out of him."

Another Case: William Wooldridge

William Wooldridge had a similar fight with the army. The specialist was hauling missiles and tank ammunition outside Baghdad when, he says, a man standing at the side of the road grabbed hold of a young girl and pushed her in front of his truck. "The little girl," Wooldridge says, his voice suddenly quiet, "she looked like one of my daughters."

When he returned to Fort Polk, Louisiana, Wooldridge told his doctor that he was now hearing voices and seeing visions, hallucinations of a mangled girl who would ask him why he had killed her. His doctor told him he had personality disorder. "When I heard that, I flew off the handle because I said, 'Hey, that ain't me. Before I went over there, I was a happy-go-lucky kind of guy.'" Wooldridge says his psychologist, Capt. [Captain] Patrick Brady of Bayne-Jones Army Community Hospital, saw him for thirty minutes before making his diagnosis. Soon after, Wooldridge was discharged from Fort Polk under Chapter 5-13.

He began to fight that discharge immediately, without success. Then in March 2005, eighteen months after Wooldridge's dismissal, his psychiatrist at the Memphis VA filed papers rejecting Brady's diagnosis and asserting that Wooldridge suffered from PTSD so severe, it made him "totally disabled." Weeks later the Army Discharge Review Board voided Wooldridge's 5-13 dismissal, but the eighteen months he'd spent lingering without benefits had already taken its toll.

"They put me out on the street to rot, and if I had left things like they were, there would have been no way I could have survived. I would have had to take myself out or had someone do it for me," he says. The way they use personality disorder to diagnose and discharge, he says, "it's like a mental rape. That's the only way I can describe it."

Captain Brady has since left Fort Polk and is now on staff at Fort Wainwright, Alaska; recently he deployed to Iraq and was unavailable for comment. In a statement, Maj. [Major] Byron Strother, chief of the Department of Behavioral Health at Bayne-Jones hospital, writes that allegations that soldiers at Fort Polk are being misdiagnosed "are not true." Strother says diagnoses at his hospital are made "only after careful consideration of all relevant clinical observation, direct examination [and] appropriate testing."

If there are dissatisfied soldiers, says Knorr, the Fort Carson official, "I'll bet not a single one of them has been diagnosed with conditions that are clear-cut and makes them medically unfit, like schizophrenia."

Chris Mosier's Case

Linda Mosier disputes that. When her son Chris left for Iraq in 2004, he was a "normal kid," she says, who'd call her long-distance and joke about the strange food and expensive taxis overseas. When he returned home for Christmas 2005, "he wouldn't sit down for a meal with us. He just kept walking around. I took him to the department store for slacks, and he was inside rushing around saying, 'Let's go, let's go, let's go.' He wouldn't sleep, and the one time he did, he woke up screaming."

Mosier told his mother of a breaking point in Iraq: a roadside bomb that blew up the truck in front of his. "He said his buddies were screaming. They were on fire," she says, her voice trailing off. "He was there at the end to pick up the hands and arms." After that Mosier started having delusions. Dr. Wexler of Fort Carson diagnosed personality disorder. Soon after, Mosier was discharged under Chapter 5-13.

Mosier returned home, still plagued by visions. In October he put a note on the front door of their Des Moines, Iowa, home saying the Iraqis were after him and he had to protect the family, then shot himself.

Mosier's mother is furious that doctors at Fort Carson treated her son for such a brief period of time and that Wexler, citing confidentiality, refused to tell her anything about that treatment or give her family any direction on how to help Chris upon his return home. She does not believe her son had a personality disorder. "They take a normal kid, he comes back messed up, then nobody was there for him when he came back," Linda says. "They discharged him so they didn't have to treat him."

Wexler did not reply to a written request seeking comment on Mosier's case.

Thrown to the Wolves

Today Jon Town is home, in small-town Findlay, Ohio, with no job, no prospects and plenty of time to reflect on how he got there. Diagnosing him with personality disorder may have saved the army thousands of dollars, he says, but what did Wexler have to gain?

Quite a lot, says Steve Robinson, director of veterans affairs at Veterans for America, a Washington, D.C.-based soldiers' rights group. Since the Iraq War began, he says, doctors have been facing an overflow of wounded soldiers and a shortage of rooms, supplies and time to treat them. By calling PTSD a personality disorder, they usher one soldier out quickly, freeing up space for the three or four who are waiting.

Terry, the veterans' advocate from IWVO, notes that unlike doctors in the private sector, army doctors who give questionable diagnoses face no danger of malpractice suits due to *Feres v. United States*, a 1950 Supreme Court ruling that bars soldiers from suing for negligence. To maintain that protection, Terry says, most doctors will diagnose personality disorder when prodded to do so by military officials.

Get Afflicted Soldiers out the Door

That's precisely how the system works, says one military official familiar with the discharge process. The official, who requested anonymity, is a lawyer with Trial Defense Service (TDS), a unit of the army that guides soldiers through their 5-13 discharge. "Commanders want to get these guys out the door and get it done fast. Even if the next soldier isn't as good, at least he's good to go. He's deployable. So they're telling the docs what diagnosis to give to get that discharge."

The lawyer says he knows this is happening because commanders have told him that they're doing it. "Some have come to me and talked about doing this. They're saying, 'Give me a specific diagnosis. It'll support a certain chapter.'"

Colonel Martin of Fort Stewart [Georgia] said the prospect of commanders pressuring doctors to diagnose personality disorder is "highly unlikely." "Doctors are making these determinations themselves," Martin says. In a statement, Col. William Statz, commander at Fort Polk's Bayne-Jones hospital, says, "Any allegations that clinical decisions are influenced by either political considerations or command pressures, at any level, are untrue."

But a second TDS lawyer, who also demanded anonymity, says he's watched the same process play out at his base. "What I've noticed is right before a unit deploys, we see a spike in 5-13s, as if the commanders are trying to clean house, get rid of the soldiers they don't really need," he says. "The chain of command just wants to eliminate them and get a new body in there fast to plug up the holes." If anyone shows even moderate signs of psychological distress, he says, "they're kicking them to the curb instead of treating them."

System Is Broken

Both lawyers say that once a commander steps in and pushes for a 5-13, the diagnosis and discharge are carved in stone fairly fast. After that happens, one lawyer says he points soldiers toward the Army Board for Correction of Military Records, where a 5-13 label could be overturned, and failing that, advises them to seek redress from their representative in Congress. Town did that, contacting Republican Representative Michael Oxley of Ohio, with little success. Oxley, who has since retired, did not return calls seeking comment.

Few cases are challenged successfully or overturned later, say the TDS lawyers. The system, says one, is essentially broken. "Right now, the army is eating its own. What I want to see is these soldiers getting the right diagnosis, so they can get the right help, not be thrown to the wolves right away. That is what they're doing."

Still, Town tries to remain undaunted. He got his story to Robinson of Veterans for America, who brought papers on his case to an October meeting with several top Washington officials, including Deputy Surgeon General Gale Pollock, Assistant Surgeon General Bernard DeKoning and Republican

Senator Kit Bond of Missouri. There Robinson laid out the larger 5-13 problem and submitted a briefing specifically on Town.

"We got a very positive response," Robinson says. "After we presented, they were almost appalled, like we are every day. They said, 'We didn't know this was happening.'" Robinson says the deputy surgeon general promised to look into Town's case and the others presented to her. Senator Bond, whose son has served in Iraq, floated the idea of a congressional hearing if the 5-13 issue isn't resolved. The senator did not return calls seeking comment.

In the meantime, Town is doing his best to keep his head in check. He says his nightmares have been waning in recent weeks, but most of his problems persist. He's thinking of going to a veterans support group in Toledo, forty-five miles north of Findlay. There will be guys there who have been through this, he says, vets who understand.

Town hesitates, his voice suddenly much softer. "I have my good days and my bad days," he says. "It all depends on whether I wake up in Findlay or Iraq."

"More than 200,000 people are fully committed to helping veterans receive the health care benefits they have earned through their service and sacrifices."

The VA Is Not Misdiagnosing Veterans in Order to Deny Benefits

Michael J. Kussman

Michael J. Kussman served as the undersecretary for health in the Department of Veterans Affairs (VA). In the following viewpoint taken from his testimony before the U.S. Senate, Kussman contends that an e-mail sent by psychologist Norma Perez suggesting that VA mental health professionals refrain from giving post-traumatic stress disorder (PTSD) diagnoses has been taken out of context and has unfairly damaged the VA's reputation. Kussman goes on to outline the programs and services the VA provides to diagnose and help soldiers and veterans suffering from PTSD.

Michael J. Kussman, Statement Before the U.S. Senate Committee on Veterans' Affairs, U.S. Senate Committee on Veterans' Affairs, June 4, 2008.

As you read, consider the following questions:

1. How much money did the VA estimate it would spend for mental health services in 2008?

2. What percentage of mental health appointments are scheduled within thirty days of the desired appointment dates nationwide?

3. What percentage of all veterans seeking mental health care are evaluated within fourteen days?

On March 20, 2008, a VA [Department of Veterans Affairs] psychologist and program coordinator for post-traumatic [stress] disorder (PTSD) sent an internal e-mail to the PTSD Clinical Treatment Team. The e-mail, as characterized by others [alleging that the VA is misdiagnosing PTSD as personality disorder to save money], does not reflect the policies or conduct of our health care system. The e-mail has been taken out of context, though we certainly agree that it could have been more artfully drafted. This is an unfortunate situation, which has also unfairly damaged the reputations of VA's dedicated and committed health care employees. The erroneous characterization may also hurt veterans and their families, as some of them may call into question the quality of VA's health care. As a result, those individuals may not seek needed medical care from the department, leaving their health care needs unaddressed. . . .

VA Gives Quality Care

VA has been, and remains, absolutely committed to delivering world-class mental health care to enrolled veterans. We are very proud of our accomplishments in this area. VA will spend more than $3.5 billion for mental health services in fiscal year (FY) 2008, and we are very proud of our accomplishments in this area. Indeed, many mental health professionals and organizations outside the department have recognized VA's leadership in this area, and I firmly believe that no one receives better mental health care in this nation than veterans enrolled in VA's health care system. This is particularly true for veterans with post-traumatic stress disorder (PTSD). VA is nationally recognized for its outstanding PTSD treatment and research programs. Although the quality of VA health care has been found equal to, and often superior to, that furnished elsewhere, the popular perception of the quality of VA care is sometimes less favorable. This is unfortunate and undeserved. Some continue to believe that health care services furnished by a government system can never be as good as those delivered by the private sector. In many cases, we have not done enough to educate the public about VA's many achievements and outstanding programs. And we could do more to ensure our own health care employees are informed about the department's recognized awards and achievements outside their own areas of expertise. VA and this country have much to be proud of in terms of the health care provided to veterans by the very skilled and talented cadre of VA clinicians, not to mention our researchers who continue to improve the clinical care veterans receive.

VA Aims to Improve Care

Improving VA's mental health services has been an active pursuit of the department for many years. In 2004, we developed a mental health strategic plan that was both unprecedented and widely acclaimed within the mental health community. Through that effort, we began to address gaps in the mental health services provided at the local level, and to initiate programs at the national level. This plan was intended to serve as a guide for four to five years. During that time, we have continually reassessed our progress and amended the strategic plan based on new information, particularly concerning new evidence-based standards of care and improvements in the delivery of mental health services. We continue to periodically re-assess the plan, as appropriate.

As alluded to earlier, the strategic plan was designed to incorporate evidence-based treatments wherever possible; encourage system redesign activities; and move our system to a recovery-based model as required by the President's [George W. Bush's] New Freedom Commission on Mental Health. For these significant changes to be successful, they must be accompanied by a major educational effort appropriately targeted at our staff and clinicians. I now believe, in retrospect, that we have not done as good a job as we should have to educate veterans and our staff.

As we have initiated new programs that emphasize recovery models for our newest veterans, we have, in some places, not adequately responded to the needs of those who use, and have benefited from, our existing programs, such as group therapy sessions for combat-theater Vietnam-era veterans. In addition, some of our own providers have not fully understood our new approach, unfortunately compounding the confusion experienced by veterans at those sites. In response, we have developed an aggressive communication and education plan for both clinicians and veterans, which will be launched in the coming weeks [mid-2008].

Communication Lapses Will Be Addressed

Be assured that despite these inadvertent, but significant, educational and communication lapses on our part, our commitment to our veterans and to improving their health status is unwavering. Their well-being and their continued improvement to full functional status has always been the objective of the strategic plan. We will work even harder to ensure we are fully sensitive to veterans' needs from this point forward and will keep them apprised of further changes based on newer evidence.

As we have always sought to do, we will do the right thing for every veteran who has entrusted us with his or her care— one veteran at a time. We will do more to make sure our decision making process for these clinical policy determinations is open and transparent to veterans. Moreover, we will work with members of this committee [U.S. Senate Committee on Veterans' Affairs], with other mental health professionals, and with veterans themselves to ensure veterans continue to receive the highest quality care available. At this time, Mr. Chairman, let me talk more generally about the status of mental health care in our department. VA strongly believes that fully addressing the physical and mental health needs of veterans is essential to their successful re-integration into civilian life. As evidence of that commitment, we plan to spend more than $3.5 billion in FY 2008 for mental health services and the president's budget has allocated $3.9 billion for that purpose in FY 2009.

Mental health care is being integrated into primary care clinics, community-based outpatient clinics, VA nursing homes, and residential care facilities. Placing mental health providers in the context of primary care for the veteran is essential; it recognizes the interrelationships of mental and physical health, and also provides mental health care at the most convenient and desirable location for the veteran.

In contrast to the private sector, whenever a veteran is seen by a VA provider, he or she is screened for PTSD, military sexual trauma, depression, and problem drinking. Screening gives us an early opportunity to assess and treat the veteran for any identified problem. Our clinicians act on positive screens, and we will continue to monitor their compliance with our national screening directives.

More Health Care Professionals to Handle the Workload

VA employs full- and part-time psychiatrists and psychologists who work in collaboration with social workers, mental health nurses, counselors, rehabilitation specialists, and other clinicians to provide a full continuum of mental health services for veterans. We have steadily increased the number of these mental health professionals over the last three years. We have hired more than 3,800 new mental health staff in that time period, for a total mental health staff of over 16,500. VA will continue expanding our mental health staff and also will continue to expand hours of operation for mental health clinics beyond normal business hours.

We have reduced wait times throughout our system. At Temple, [a Texas VA facility] for example, 99.58 percent of all mental health appointments are within 30 days of the desired appointment date. Nationwide, the percentage is 99.34 percent—and for veterans with PTSD, the percentage rises to 99.66 percent. We've also set standards for timeliness in our compensation and pension examinations. Nationally, our average in March [was] 28 days to process these exams; Network 17, in which Temple is located, processed exams in 22 days.

VA Provides Follow-up

Our department will continue to aggressively follow up on patients in mental health and substance abuse programs who miss appointments to ensure they do not miss needed, additional care. VA will also continue to monitor the standards the Veterans Health Administration [VHA] has set for itself: to provide initial evaluations of all patients with mental health issues within 24 hours, to provide urgent care immediately when that evaluation indicates it is needed, and to complete a full evaluation and initiate a treatment plan within 14 days for those not needing immediate crisis care. At present, 93.4 percent of all veterans seeking mental health care receive full evaluations within 14 days. VISN [Veterans Integrated Service Network] 17 has a percentage exactly equal to the national average.

On May 1, VA began contacting nearly 570,000 combat veterans of the global war on terror to ensure they know about VA medical services and other benefits. The department

Pressure Not to Diagnose PTSD at the Department of Veterans Affairs (VA)

In spring 2008, psychologist Norma Perez, who at the time was the coordinator of a PTSD [post-traumatic stress disorder] clinical team in a Texas VA medical center, sent an e-mail to staff with the subject "Suggestion." Perez stated that "given we are having more and more compensation seeking veterans, I'd like to suggest that you refrain from giving a diagnosis of PTSD straight out. Consider a diagnosis of adjustment disorder. . . . Additionally, we really don't have time to do the extensive testing that should be done to determine PTSD."

Scientific Integrity,
"Pressure Not to Diagnose PTSD at the U.S. Army and Department of Veterans Affairs," November 9, 2009.

will reach out to every veteran of the war to let them know we are here for them. Last month, we completed calls to more than 15,000 veterans who were sick or injured while serving in Iraq or Afghanistan. If any of these 15,000 veterans do not now have a care manager to work with them to ensure they receive appropriate health care, VA offered to appoint one for them.

While the numbers of veterans seeking VA care for PTSD is increasing, VA is monitoring parameters (such as time to first appointment for new and established veterans of all service eras) to ensure they receive prompt and efficient services for PTSD and other mental disorders. In FY 2009, funding enhancements will close gaps in services and allow us to implement a more comprehensive and uniform package of clinical services for PTSD and other disorders. . . .

VA Suicide Prevention Programs

Further, VA is taking significant steps to prevent suicide among veterans. We have provided training to all VA employees to underscore that even strong and normally resilient people can develop mental health conditions making them susceptible to suicide; care for those conditions is readily available and should be immediately provided; and treatment typically works.

VA's suicide prevention program includes two centers that conduct research and provide technical assistance in this area to all locations of care. One is the Mental Health Center of Excellence in Canandaigua, New York, which focuses on developing and testing clinical and public health intervention related to suicide risk and prevention. The other is the VISN 19 Mental Illness Research Education and Clinical Center in Denver, which focuses on research in the clinical and neurobiological sciences with special emphasis on issues related to suicide risk.

VA has opened a unique suicide prevention call center in Canandaigua focused entirely on veterans. Suicide prevention coordinators are located at each of VA's 153 hospitals. Altogether, VA has more than 200 mental health providers whose jobs are specifically devoted to preventing suicide among veterans.

In developing the suicide prevention call center, the department has partnered with the Lifeline program of the Substance Abuse and Mental Health Services Administration. Those who call 1-800-273-TALK are asked to press "1" if they are a veteran, or are calling about a veteran.

From its beginnings in July 2007 through the end of April, 16,414 calls have come to the hotline from veterans and 2,125 family members or friends have called on behalf of a loved one. These calls have led to 3,464 referrals to suicide prevention coordinators and 885 rescues involving emergency services. Of note, 493 active-duty service members have also called our suicide hotline. Unlike other such hotlines, VA's hotline is staffed solely by mental health professionals—24 hours a day, seven days a week. Our hotline staff is trained in both crisis intervention strategies, and in issues relating specifically to veterans, such as traumatic brain injury and post-traumatic stress disorder. In emergencies, the hotline staff contacts local emergency resources, such as police or ambulance services, to ensure an immediate response.

If the veteran is a VA patient and willing to identify himself or herself, the hotline staff is able to access the veteran's electronic medical record during the call. These records provide information that is invaluable during a crisis, including information on medications; the patient's treatment plan; and names and numbers of persons to contact during this emergency. VA hotline staff can also talk directly to the facility that is treating the veteran. They can place consults in the patient's medical record. For veterans not under VA care, staff can refer them to an individual VA medical center or community-based outpatient clinic as appropriate, and see to all of the necessary administrative requirements.

And our hotline staff follows up on these referrals. They also check patients' records to see if consultations were completed and to ensure follow-up actions were taken or are ongoing. If the record does not show this information, the suicide prevention coordinator at the VA facility is called and tasked with following up on the case to ensure that no referral is lost in the process.

Outreach and Counseling Services

In addition to the care offered in medical centers and community-based outpatient clinics, VA's Vet Centers provide outreach and readjustment counseling services to returning combat-theater veterans of all eras. It is well established that rehabilitation for war-related PTSD, substance use disorder, and other military-related readjustment problems, along with the treatment of the physical wounds of war, is central to VA's continuum of health care programs specific to the needs of combat-theater veterans.

The Vet Centers' mission is to provide readjustment and related mental health services, through a holistic mix of services designed to treat the veteran as a whole person in his/her community setting. Vet Centers provide an alternative to traditional mental health care that helps many combat-theater veterans overcome the stigma and fear related to accessing professional assistance for military-related problems. Vet Centers are staffed by interdisciplinary teams that include psychologists, nurses and social workers, many of whom are veteran peers.

Vet Centers provide professional readjustment counseling for war-related psychological readjustment problems, including PTSD. Other readjustment problems may include family relationship problems, lack of adequate employment, lack of educational achievement, social alienation and lack of career goals, homelessness and lack of adequate resources, and other psychological problems such as depression and/or substance use disorder. Vet Centers also provide military-related sexual trauma counseling, bereavement counseling, employment counseling and job referrals, preventive health care information, and referrals to other VA and non-VA medical and benefits facilities. . . .

I am very proud of what VHA does in the area of mental health care. More than 200,000 people are fully committed to helping veterans receive the health care benefits they have earned through their service and sacrifices. I hope we can continue to move forward from this episode and help veterans and their families; Congress; the news media and others to better understand what VA has done, and is doing, to fulfill our nation's commitment to those who have worn the uniform of our armed services.

> *"Our Vietnam experience doesn't just
> tell us that some vets will be afflicted
> with mental illness, it also tells us that
> if we aren't careful we can make the
> problem worse."*

Post-Traumatic Stress
Disorder Is Over-Diagnosed

Sally Satel

*Sally Satel is a scholar at the American Enterprise Institute for
Public Policy Research and co-author of* One Nation Under
Therapy: How the Helping Culture Is Eroding Self-Reliance.
*In the following viewpoint, she states that from her experience
working as a psychiatrist at a Department of Veterans Affairs
(VA) hospital, many of the veterans diagnosed with post-
traumatic stress disorder (PTSD) have been misdiagnosed and
could have been rehabilitated. Satel argues that disability payments become a trap and discourage troubled veterans from improving.*

As you read, consider the following questions:

1. As of 2005, how many veterans does the VA classify as
   disabled by PTSD?

Sally Satel, "Saving Our Vets Once They're Home: The Right Kind of Mental Health
Treatment Is Vital," *Los Angeles Times*, June 13, 2005. Reproduced by permission of the
author.

2. What is the first thing the VA can do to avoid creating a "new generation" of chronically ill veterans, according to Satel?

3. Why should the VA emphasize "reintegration" with returning veterans, in the author's opinion?

"The mental toll that this war has had on our newest generation of veterans ... could well be my generation's Agent Orange [a contaminated herbicide that harmed soldiers in Vietnam] syndrome." That's the head of the nation's largest advocacy group for Iraq war veterans, Operation Truth, speaking.

He's not alone in his concerns. Rep. [Representative] Lane Evans (D-Ill.) has sponsored legislation to increase federal spending on mental health treatment for our troops, because, he says, returning soldiers could suffer post-traumatic stress disorder [PTSD] at rates "roughly comparable" to Vietnam War veterans.

Of course, it's true that some soldiers will return from Iraq and Afghanistan with severe psychological problems, and we must do everything to help them. But our Vietnam experience doesn't just tell us that some vets will be afflicted with mental illness, it also tells us that if we aren't careful we can make the problem worse.

The issue is chronicity. As Evans says, "Quick intervention and ready access to services are keys to ensuring that an acute stress reaction does not become a chronic one."

Providing the Right Treatment

I worked as a psychiatrist at a Veterans Affairs [VA] hospital in Connecticut for five years in the late '80s and early '90s. Unsettling as this sounds, I believe a sizable number of the roughly 224,000 veterans that the VA counts today [in 2005] as being disabled by post-traumatic stress disorder could have been rehabilitated.

Symptoms of Post-Traumatic Stress Disorder (PTSD)

1. Re-experiencing symptoms:

- Flashbacks—reliving the trauma over and over, including physical symptoms like a racing heart or sweating.
- Bad dreams.
- Frightening thoughts.

Re-experiencing symptoms may cause problems in a person's everyday routine. . . .

2. Avoidance symptoms:

- Staying away from places, events, or objects that are reminders of the experience.
- Feeling emotionally numb.
- Feeling strong guilt, depression, or worry.
- Losing interest in activities that were enjoyable in the past.
- Having trouble remembering the dangerous event.

Things that remind a person of the traumatic event can trigger avoidance symptoms. These symptoms may cause a person to change his or her personal routine. . . .

3. Hyperarousal symptoms:

- Being easily startled.
- Feeling tense or "on edge."
- Having difficulty sleeping, and/or having angry outbursts.

National Institute of Mental Health,
"What Are the Symptoms of PTSD?"
Nimh.nih.gov, January 21, 2009.

Despite good intentions, the agency itself almost certainly played a role in many veterans becoming lasting psychiatric casualties of war.

This resulted from a confluence of unfortunate practices. First, VA mental health workers commonly believed—and many still do—that participation in war results, de facto, in post-traumatic stress disorder. In communicating this mistaken notion to veterans, they set up expectations of illness. Second, treatments themselves inadvertently contributed to problems. Third, generous VA disability payments may act as a disincentive to recovery.

How can the VA avoid creating a "new generation" of chronically ill vets? It can start by carefully interpreting psychological states. Many soldiers returning from war will feel confused, sad. They may have trouble sleeping, be easily distracted, and some will be bitter, even hostile. Whether this is psychopathology depends on how impaired they are and the persistence of the problem. It is vital to remember, however, that people in a fragile state can be susceptible to the suggestion that they are ill, and latch on to that idea.

Conversely, when otherwise healthy men and women are told they are experiencing natural and time-limited reentry difficulties, they will generally adopt that outlook.

The VA must also emphasize "reintegration."

Smoothly adjusting to family and community life depends largely on a veteran's economic security, family stability and physical health. Rehabilitation and social services are key. Such support can also help veterans regard their service as a worthy sacrifice or put their regret or guilt into perspective. They will suffer less than those who remain isolated and demoralized.

Another lesson is to keep treatment practical. Standard care for Vietnam War vets entailed months-long inpatient stays in special units. That increased identification with invalidism and made readjustment to civilian life harder. Therapy often consisted of repeatedly telling war stories to release anger and sadness. For many this exacerbated their problems. As the VA now recognizes, hospitalization should be reserved for those who can't function in another environment.

It's Okay to Be Skeptical

Unfortunately, experience shows that the VA must be skeptical about claims of combat-related distress. In a report this month [June 2005] in the *British Journal of Psychiatry*, researchers at a South Carolina VA facility checked the backgrounds of 100 Vietnam War vets being treated for combat-related post-traumatic stress disorder. They could not confirm combat exposure for 59% of them.

Finally, the VA must beware of the disability trap: Veterans should not be urged to obtain long-term disability payments for at least two years after their return from overseas. In most circumstances, psychiatric conditions will be temporary. Moreover, generous disability payments provide an economic incentive to remain ill. In fact, work is often good therapy, providing structure, a sense of purpose and social opportunities.

The VA and mental health workers will do returning war veterans a disservice if their care isn't handled correctly. As my colleague, British psychiatrist Simon Wessely, says: "Generals are justly criticized for fighting the last war, not the present one. Psychiatrists should be aware of the same mistake."

| *"Enter [traumatic brain injury], which doesn't always render a person physically disabled and fully dependent but if left untreated, can devastate lives."*

Veterans with Traumatic Brain Injuries Are Being Neglected

Kelley Beaucar Vlahos

Kelley Beaucar Vlahos is a reporter based in Washington, D.C. In the following viewpoint, she maintains that traumatic brain injury (TBI) is a growing problem with Iraq and Afghanistan veterans because it is often misdiagnosed and takes time to show symptoms in full. Vlahos argues that there is not enough screening and treatment for those suffering from TBI, and she describes the condition of life for some veterans neglected by the Department of Veterans Affairs.

As you read, consider the following questions:

1. What are some symptoms of TBI that Vlahos identifies?

2. According to Paul Sullivan's estimates, how many service members and veterans are suffering from some degree of TBI?

3. How many of the 1.4 million service members who have served in Iraq and Afghanistan have been exposed to a bomb blast or other head trauma?

When Samuel Vaughan Wilson III speaks, he periodically stops mid-sentence to rub his jaw, still pained by the rocket-propelled grenade [RPG] that ripped through his vehicle, grazing his face and singeing the nerves inside his mouth. It was one of several close calls during that year in Afghanistan: After one IED [improvised explosive device] attack, he recalls with a medic's precision how, under heavy gunfire, he cut open an Afghan police officer's throat to clear an air passage, saving his life. He says with equal sobriety that his army career is over.

"My father wants me to get screening [for traumatic brain injury]. He thinks something is wrong," said Wilson, who served as a combat medic in Afghanistan with the 508th Parachute Infantry, survived four IED incidents, numerous firefights, and that RPG near miss. According to the recommendation for his Army Commendation Medal, Wilson was credited, in one incident, with saving eight lives and maintaining his composure under "the most extreme circumstances in a combat environment." But in September 2006, he left the military after 11 years under a rare medical discharge for post-traumatic stress disorder [PTSD].

Struggling to Identify the Problem

He now struggles to understand where his physical injuries leave off and the mental ones begin. His anger, restlessness, and sleepless nights are classic symptoms of both mild TBI [traumatic brain injury] and PTSD, which are provoked regularly during his day job as an emergency paramedic in northern Virginia. "We've looked into it," he said, of possible TBI screening, "but I've gotten nowhere in the VA [Department of Veterans Affairs] system yet."

Red-headed Wilson, 36, says he looks like Howdy Doody, but nothing about him is funny. The black ID bracelet of a platoon mate killed in action firmly around his wrist, he is at one turn intimidating and dark, at another vulnerable, self-deprecating, and visibly wracked with survivor's guilt. He's outrun death, but doesn't quite feel alive.

"I love the army—I was born and raised in it," Wilson said, reflecting, not for the first time, on his lineage, which includes a grandfather, (Ret.) Lt. Gen. [Retired Lieutenant General] Samuel Vaughan Wilson Sr., who as one of "Merrill's Marauders" fought behind enemy lines in Burma in World War II. The grandson isn't the first in his family to bring home PTSD along with medals for valor. His haunted nocturnal pacing when he returned from Afghanistan forced his father, (Ret.) Army Lt. Col. [Retired Army Lieutenant Colonel] Samuel Vaughan Wilson Jr., to face down a reappearance of his own demons, left over from the rice paddy wars a generation ago.

"He and I walked in each other's shoes if you will. His war was very similar to mine in that we both dealt with combat that was asymmetrical—at the least expected moments, [the fighting] would flare up," said the elder Wilson, an infantry officer in Vietnam in the early 1970s.

But one major difference between his war in the Mekong Delta and his son's in Kandahar is that, thanks to improvements in body armor and emergency medical response, today the military is bringing more soldiers and marines home alive—battered, shattered, and transformed, but not in the body bags that drove a nation to disenchanted departure from Southeast Asia.

The Horror of TBI

Yet by the thousands, they are also returning with horrifying injuries, the most pervasive being the IED's especially vicious souvenir: traumatic brain injury. Symptoms range from memory loss, fatigue, irritability, mood swings, and a change in sleep patterns in milder cases to loss of coordination and balance, seizures, migraines, confusion, and agitation in more severe instances.

"TBI is going to be the worst story in terms of returning veterans," said Paul Sullivan, an advocate with Veterans for America. He estimates that anywhere from 160,000 to 320,000 service members and veterans are suffering from some degree of TBI today [in mid-2007], "most of which are unscreened, undiagnosed, and untreated."

Wilson's story is hardly rare. Physically, soldiers like him look healthy, but they come home changed, confused about their circumstances and often too ashamed to seek help. If they are still on active duty, they worry that their brain injury or PTSD will be mistaken for a preexisting personality disorder, which could result in a bad discharge. They are anxious about getting a good disability rating when they leave the military, as statistics show the army is low-balling ratings for PTSD, TBI, and other injuries, meaning there is a good chance all they will get from Uncle Sam is a severance check.

Once out, they face a long waiting list at the Veterans' Administration [currently the Department of Veterans Affairs (VA)] and a lack of mental health care access in rural areas. Many contemplate or commit suicide, get divorced, leave their jobs, and even walk the streets, homeless.

"The idea of okay, cheer them up, wave the flag, bring them home, and forget about them . . . we're going to be paying for this for the rest of their lives. It's going to be a horrible bill that we're going to pay," said Wilson's dad, now a high school teacher in quiet Farmville, Virginia.

"If we've got any moral virtue left, we've got to pay it," he added. "We really didn't anticipate, as a country, and as a nation, the tremendous stresses on our medical system. It's a horrible thing."

Warriors for the Wounded

But some people did anticipate it, and veterans from previous and current wars—call them "warriors for the wounded"— have been working endlessly and aggressively to ensure today's veteran isn't betrayed.

Take Sullivan, a Gulf War veteran who left his job as a senior researcher at the VA in March 2006, frustrated his distress signals were being ignored. "They went on record with the *Boston Globe* that I was 'alarmist,'" he said of a March feature on the perils of the VA system. "I had no other choice but to pull the alarm." The VA does not refute Sullivan's research but winces at his interpretation.

With an estimated 5.5 million veterans being treated at the nation's 1,400 hospitals and clinics each year—230,000 of them from Afghanistan and Iraq—and an estimated 470,000 more yet to move into a system that is experiencing a backlog of 400,000 disability claims and a six-month average wait for a medical appointment, it is hard not [to] see fire on the mountain.

"Everyone is giving lip service, but Walter Reed is just the tip of the iceberg," Sullivan said, referring to the recent scandal at Walter Reed Army Medical Center, where soldiers were found languishing in moldy conditions, outflanked by a seemingly unsympathetic bureaucracy. Surveying the hundreds of thousands of new claims coming in, staff shortages, inefficiencies, and the increased needs of older veterans, he declares, "The VA is in a crisis right now."

TBI Emerges Slowly

Enter TBI, which doesn't always render a person physically disabled and fully dependent but if left untreated, can devastate lives. Thousands of times in this war soldiers close to a bomb blast have shaken themselves off and walked away to patrol another day. Months later, they return home and do not recognize the face in the mirror.

"It's like slamming a laptop against the wall," said Patrick Campbell, 29, a National Guardsman who served in the 256th Infantry Brigade as a medic in Iraq from November 2004 to October 2005. While the computer may seem functional afterwards, small quirks like a broken backspace key or a jagged line down one side of the screen soon become obvious and render use slow, frustrating, and intolerable for the long term.

"The concussive event—the wind and the pressure changes—it's more damaging than the force of getting hit," said Campbell.

He will tell you that in a single incident, an IED explosion causes an intense shockwave of pressure. When close enough, it can form tiny, destructive air bubbles in the brain and blow out precious wiring inside a soldier's skull. Those not affected by the blast wave may be hurtled through the air, slammed around in a vehicle, or hit in the head with debris. Their Humvee [vehicle] might overturn. As described by some, any of this could throttle the brains like Jell-O.

In Vietnam, one soldier was killed for every 2.5 wounded; in Iraq the survival rate is one killed for every 16 wounded. But the effects of TBI may take hours, days—even weeks—to surface.

Spreading the News About TBI

While at first glance Campbell looks as if he would be more comfortable in an armored Humvee than a downtown D.C. office space, it's soon clear his new posting is a good fit. Working full-time for the Iraq and Afghanistan Veterans of America [IAVA], which is steadily becoming the generational equivalent of such scrappy advocates as the National Gulf War Resource Center or Vietnam Veterans of America, his goal is to cast a floodlight on TBI's effect on returning service members.

"There are a lot of people out there who have never been 'right' after an IED," said Campbell, recalling one case in which a veteran had to carry around a notebook to write down everything he did, said, or had to accomplish because his short-term memory was shot. "Now they are at home and wondering why they are different."

He recalls his own multiple "concussive events" in Iraq. One, an IED blast, left his ears bleeding and he and his buddy laughing over their luck. He went right back on patrol. Today, he plans to take advantage of the new mandatory TBI screening at the VA, wondering if those events contributed to his own diagnosis of PTSD.

"Not all people want to acknowledge that they have a problem. The symptoms are extremely close to PTSD," which still carries a stigma, particularly among peers and the chain of command. It took Campbell a year and losing his best friend over his changed personality to finally seek help.

TBI Screenings

Thanks to lobbying efforts by groups like the IAVA, the VA announced in April that it will begin screening all incoming veterans from Iraq and Afghanistan for TBI. Now the pressure is on the Department of Defense, which only offers comprehensive TBI screening for the wounded coming into their hospitals, like Walter Reed.

If TBI is the silent affliction of this war, the casualty count should be the canary in the coal mine. As of mid-May, the military in Iraq suffered 14,804 injuries that required medical transport off the battlefield. This included 7,628 combat wounded and 7,176 non-hostile injuries, plus 19,589 "diseases," which cover everything from a bacterial infection and mental disorder to cancer and pregnancy, that also required medical air transport. In Afghanistan, 6,213 injured soldiers were evacuated from the field, including 743 combat-related, 1,458 non-hostile, and 4,012 diseases.

Symptoms of TBI can turn up in any of the these categories. According to various reports, of the 1.4 million who have rotated through Iraq and Afghanistan, anywhere from 10 to

© 2007 RJ Matson, Roll Call and PoliticalCartoons.com.

30 percent have been exposed to a bomb blast or other head trauma, leaving them with at least mild TBI. A recent study by doctors at Fort Carson army base in Colorado found that 18 percent of their returning soldiers had incurred a brain injury in Iraq.

No One Knows the Scope of TBI

Some 60 percent of the veterans in the VA's Polytrauma Rehabilitation Center in Tampa, Florida, one of 21 centers handling vets with severe, multiple injuries, have a brain injury, according to ABC newsman Bob Woodruff in a February series he put together after his own year-long recovery from an IED blast. Meanwhile, officials at the Defense and Veterans

Brain Injury Center [DVBIC], the military's primary research and treatment facility for TBI, has treated 2,130 patients since 2003.

"That's just a small percentage of the total number, and the fact is, nobody really knows how many have mild [TBI]," said Col. Jonathan Jaffin, commander of U.S Army Medical Research and Materiel Command at Fort Detrick, Maryland, and a spokesman for the DVBIC. He said 70 percent of their cases are mild and those affected may, with the right treatment, recover or at least adjust to their disabilities. But it is not clear, according to doctors, how soldiers with cumulative concussive injuries will fare long term. All seem to agree the body of research on nonfatal blast injuries is thin.

"Mild head injury for years had been somewhat neglected," Jaffin says, with standard testing for TBI often missing less severe cases. "So people would be suffering and being told they are normal." As the pervasiveness of TBI among returning service members became clear, he said, the military and VA began developing better ways to detect it—though advocates will dispute their commitment.

VA officials say they are treating nearly 400 veterans diagnosed with moderate to severe TBI, while overall they have seen more than 1,600 potential cases since 2002. They acknowledge, however, that the system has yet to compile statistics for mild cases or outpatients.

Misdiagnosing TBI Is Common

Meanwhile, symptoms of mild to moderate TBI go unchecked, crowded out by the more obvious injuries. Furthermore, misdiagnosing TBI—most likely mistaken for PTSD—is commonplace.

"When it does occur, PTSD and TBI together can be especially difficult to spot. The problem lies in the overlapping symptoms—increased anxiety, short attention span, limited concentration, problems with memory. This overlap muddles things up," points out Ilona Meagher, author of *Moving a Nation to Care: Post-Traumatic Stress Disorder and America's Returning Troops.* "Once you have these kinds of errors on military records," she added, "it creates a whole other level of problems down the road for the veteran after they've returned home."

That road is paved with the stories of men and women who find that the system is no more compassionate than it was for their counterparts returning from Vietnam a generation ago. The PTSD label is not only stigmatizing, but its symptoms are often mistaken for personality disorders and are blamed for behavioral problems like insubordination and substance abuse, resulting in a one-way ticket out of the military with no retirement pay or benefits.

"This time it's all about money—they just don't want to pay," insists Sullivan. But unlike previous wars, there is a small army of veterans advocates, many who cut their teeth on behalf of Persian Gulf soldiers in the 1990s.

A Pattern of Misdiagnoses

Steve Robinson, also with Veterans for America, packed his experience and reputation along with his bags and spent most of May around Fort Carson, pulling together a massive case accusing the command of erroneously discharging 276 soldiers for personality disorders. These service members all suffered from PTSD, and many had accompanying TBI diagnoses. His organization is also investigating more than 40 current cases on the base. They include bad discharges but also complaints from soldiers that their brain injuries and mental health problems were mishandled or ignored by superiors.

Robinson, who has been working tirelessly as an advocate since his own stint in the Persian Gulf War, helped to attract a delegation of congressional staff who met in a closed-door briefing with spouses. His work also brought on a Government Accountability Office probe.

Spc. [Specialist] Paul Thurman, 24, is part of that investigation. After two head injuries incurred during training at Fort Bragg [North Carolina] and in Kuwait, even under heavy medication he struggles daily with uncontrollable shaking, intense headaches, short-term memory loss, twitching, and the threat of seizures. His moment of terror came when he suffered a seizure and threw up during a meeting with an army lawyer.

He was waiting for his medical evaluation and discharge at Fort Carson when he was given an Article 15—the nonjudicial punishment meted out by a commander for minor disciplinary offenses—for cussing and walking off formation when he was told he couldn't get his seizure medication at the onset of an episode.

Robinson and company took up Thurman's case because they say he should not have been deployed after the first head injury. He had been diagnosed with lesions on the brain. "These guys came forward and said, look, you can't push this dude around. They've been unbelievably helpful," Thurman said of Robinson's crew. "They know how to care for us."

Thurman's only mode of transportation before he joined the military at the age of 18 was a bicycle. He thought, cycling daily past the recruitment center, that the service would give him a job and his life direction. Now he can't find a job because he can't drive a car and the seizures aren't a selling point with employers. He's tired of the emergency room—particularly how he is made to feel that he's done something wrong—and he's scared that talking about it will put his final discharge status at risk.

A System-Wide Problem

Fort Carson says there is another side to these stories. While the base hasn't denied struggling with TBI and PTSD—which according to reports has increased from 32 cases to 539 in the last year there—officials say none or the soldiers chaptered out for personality disorders were suffering from severe PTSD or TBI. Rather, their behavior, backed by a preexisting condition found in their backgrounds, got them booted.

Robinson said his group chose Fort Carson as the first in five fact-finding missions because it had the most documentation to back up the soldiers' claims. However, "these problems are system-wide."

> "[President] Obama recognized that thousands of Iraq and Afghanistan veterans have suffered from traumatic brain injury, and said the budget will provide improved services for these cognitive injuries."

The VA Is Increasing Funding for Programs for Veterans Suffering from Traumatic Brain Injury

Donna Miles

Donna Miles is a reporter for American Forces Press Service. In the following viewpoint, she reports on a funding request of the Department of Veterans Affairs (VA) that will provide additional post-traumatic stress disorder (PTDS) and traumatic brain injury (TBI) services to combat veterans. Miles relates President Barack Obama's commitment to treating veterans afflicted with mental health injuries, particularly TBI.

As you read, consider the following questions:

1. How much will the budget increase from 2009 to 2014, according to Miles?

Donna Miles, "VA Budget Adds Mental-Health Services for Returning Combat Vets," American Forces Press Service, April 9, 2009.

2. According to President Obama, how many more veterans will receive benefits because of additional funding?

3. How will the funding increase help homeless veterans, according to the viewpoint?

The proposed Department of Veterans Affairs [VA] funding request will provide more post-traumatic stress disorder [PTSD] and traumatic brain injury [TBI] services to combat veterans, as well as other mental health care and services for wounded warriors, President Barack Obama said today [April 9, 2009].

"The nightmares of war don't always end when our loved ones return home," Obama said. "Untold thousands of servicemen and women returning from Iraq and Afghanistan suffer from post-traumatic stress disorder or other serious psychological injury."

The president called the growing incidence of suicide among active-duty service members and returning combat veterans "disturbing."

"Sometimes the deadliest wounds are the ones you cannot see, and we cannot afford to let the unseen wounds go untreated," he said. "And that's why this budget dramatically increases funding for mental health screening and treatment at all levels."

A Needed Increase

The proposed budget represents the largest single-year increase in VA funding in three decades. "All told, we will increase funding by $25 billion over the next five years," the president said.

Obama recognized that thousands of Iraq and Afghanistan veterans have suffered from traumatic brain injury, and said the budget will provide improved services for these cognitive injuries.

The Estimated Increase in Benefits for Veterans

Projected number of veterans to receive benefits for traumatic brain injuries

Year	Number	Annual Cost
2009	3,546	$10.08 million
2010	3,746	$10.14 million
2011	3,946	$11.1 million
2012	4,146	$12.1 million
2013	4,346	$13.1 million
2014	4,546	$14.2 million
2015	4,746	$15.3 million
2016	4,946	$16.5 million
2017	5,146	$17.7 million

Source: Department of Veterans Affairs.

TAKEN FROM: Gregg Zoroya, "VA to Increase Benefits for Mild Brain Trauma," *USA Today*, September 23, 2008.

"Many with TBI have never been evaluated by a physician," he said. "And because such injuries can often have long-term impacts that only show up down the road, this funding will help ensure they received the ongoing care they need."

The budget proposal also will increase the number of Vet Centers and mobile health clinics, expanding access to mental health care in rural areas, he said. Meanwhile, it also aims to reduce the stigma of seeking care by adding mental health professionals to educate veterans and their families about their injuries and their options.

In addition to more comprehensive mental health services, Obama said the funding request will provide other improvements in the medical care and other benefits veterans receive.

"This budget doesn't just signify increased funding for the VA health care program," he said. "It significantly expands coverage so that 500,000 more veterans who have previously been denied it will receive it, and it strengthens care and services across a broad range of areas."

The proposed budget also will:

- Invest in better technology to deliver services and benefits to veterans with the quality and efficiency they deserve;

- Provide greater benefits to veterans who are medically retired from service;

- Combat homelessness by safeguarding vulnerable veterans; and

- Ensure the timely adoption of new, comprehensive education benefits that veterans earn through their military service.

Fighting Homelessness

Obama said all Americans "share the shame of 154,000 veterans going homeless on any given night."

His budget request will fund a pilot program for not-for-profit groups to ensure that veterans at risk of losing their homes have a roof over their heads. "And we will not rest until we reach a day when not one single veteran falls into homelessness," he said.

Obama also expressed optimism over Senate support for a measure that would provide advanced medical care funding for veterans.

"The care that our veterans receive should never be hindered by budget delays," Obama said, adding that the plan he and VA Secretary Eric K. Shinseki have advanced will ensure there's no disruption.

"What that means is a timely and predictable flow of funding from year to year, but more importantly, that means better care for our veterans," he said.

Periodical Bibliography

The following articles have been selected to supplement the diverse views presented in this chapter.

Lizette Alvarez and Erik Eckholm	"Purple Heart Is Ruled Out for PTSD," *New York Times*, January 7, 2009.
Mark Benjamin and Michael de Yoanna	"'I Believe That I Did Have PTSD,'" Salon.com, April 10, 2009. www.salon.com.
John J. Dilulio Jr.	"The Wacko-Vet Myth," *Weekly Standard*, January 14, 2008.
Bruce Falconer	"Agent Orange: Treatment for Vets Still Lagging, Says Report," *Mother Jones*, June 1, 2009.
New Scientist	"Concussed, Stressed, or Just Sick of War?" April 28, 2009.
Jamie Reno	"PTSD: New War on an Old Foe," *Newsweek*, October 1, 2009.
Robert P. Salvatore	"Posttraumatic Stress Disorder: A Treatable Public Health Problem," *Health & Social Work*, May 1, 2009.
Stephen Soldz	"Diagnostic Abuse of Veterans," *CounterPunch*, April 9, 2009.
Mark Thompson	"Study Points to a Clear-Cut Way to Diagnose PTSD," *Time*, January 25, 2010.
Michael Weisskopf	"Veterans Day in Court," *Time*, January 12, 2008.

OPPOSING
VIEWPOINTS®
SERIES

CHAPTER 4

How Can the U.S. Government Help Veterans?

Chapter Preface

The GI Bill, also known as the Servicemen's Readjustment Act, enacted in 1944, provided a range of benefits for veterans returning from service after World War II, including college or vocational education, unemployment compensation, and loans to buy homes and start businesses. The GI Bill of 1944 is acknowledged to be an unqualified success: Before the war, it would have been very difficult for the average American to afford a college education, buy a house, or start a business. Because of the benefits offered in the GI Bill, however, returning veterans had access to these things—especially the pursuit of higher education. In 1947 veterans accounted for 49 percent of college admissions. By the time the GI Bill ran out on July 25, 1956, 7.8 million World War II veterans had taken advantage of the college or vocational education offered by the bill.

Equally successful was the GI Bill's home loan guaranty. From 1944 to 1952, returning World War II veterans were given 2.4 million home loans guaranteed by the U.S. government. Scholars attribute much of the American postwar economic boom to the generous benefits of the GI Bill, which allowed veterans to pursue their dreams and catapulted the American economy to global prominence.

In 1984 the GI Bill was overhauled by former Mississippi congressman Gillespie V. "Sonny" Montgomery. The bill, known as the Montgomery GI Bill, expanded and enhanced popular veterans benefits, particularly the educational programs and home loan guaranty.

As veterans of the Iraq and Afghanistan wars began to return home, calls for another revamping of the GI Bill were heard. Supporters of a new GI bill argued that the educational benefits of the Montgomery bill were far inferior to those available to World War II veterans. For example, it was reported that the 2007 GI bill covered less than 70 percent of the average tuition cost at a four-year college and less than two years at a private college. In addition, National Guardsmen and Reservists were eligible for only a fraction of that. Supporters of the new bill asserted that improving benefits for veterans would not only stimulate a moribund U.S. economy, but would also help veterans build better lives and achieve the American dream—just as their predecessors did after World War II.

Critics of a new GI bill argued that today's veterans are paid competitive salaries with generous signing bonuses, and could take advantage of very good educational programs. Some critics maintained that by providing improved educational benefits, the U.S. government would be hindering the all-volunteer force—that instead of reenlisting, soldiers would leave to take advantage of new and enhanced tuition benefits.

On June 30, 2008, the Post-9/11 GI Bill, or the Post-9/11 Veterans Educational Assistance Act, became law. Proposed by Virginia senator Jim Webb, the new GI bill expanded the educational benefits for veterans who have served since September 11, 2001. The new law provides 100 percent funding of a public four-year undergraduate education to a veteran who has served three years on active duty since September 11, 2001, and it allows veterans to transfer benefits to a spouse or children after serving (or making the commitment to serve) ten years in the military.

The debate over the new GI bill is one of the subjects examined in this chapter. Other viewpoints explore the viability of applying the successes of the health care system of the Department of Veterans Affairs (VA) to the larger process of U.S. health care reform as well as finding a better way to fund the VA health system.

| "Once health care funding matches the actual average cost of care for the veterans enrolled in the system, with annual indexing for inflation, VA can truly fulfill its mission."

Assured Public Funding Is the Best Way to Fund VA Services

William A. Boettcher

William A. Boettcher is the national commander of American Veterans or AMVETS, an organization that provides services for veterans. In the following viewpoint taken from testimony in front of a joint session of the Senate Committee on Veterans' Affairs, he argues that the current funding system of the Department of Veterans Affairs (VA) is broken, and he urges Congress to adopt assured funding of VA health care. Boettcher believes that assured funding will help the VA match its actual funding to the average cost of care for enrolled veterans.

As you read, consider the following questions:

1. How have VA funding shortfalls affected Denver's veterans' hospital, according to Boettcher?

William Boettcher, Statement Before a Joint Session of the Committee on Veterans' Affairs, U.S. Senate Committee on Veterans' Affairs, April 14, 2005. Reproduced by permission of the author.

2. What was the 2005 national budget?

3. What does Boettcher cite as projects that received funding while the VA is underfunded?

AMVETS [American Veterans] has been a leader since 1944 in helping to preserve the freedoms secured by America's armed forces. Through our national scholarship program, AMVETS has awarded more than $2 million in scholarships to graduating high school students. For the past 17 years, we have sponsored a high school youth leadership program in cooperation with Freedoms Foundation at Valley Forge. Last year [2004], AMVETS, its [National] Ladies Auxiliary and [National] Sons organizations contributed nearly a quarter million hours of voluntary service, helping veterans and providing an array of community services that enhance the quality of life for our nation's citizens.

Veterans Are Owed Our Gratitude

As a national veterans service organization, AMVETS believes as President [George W.] Bush said at Arlington National Cemetery, "We owe our veterans the life we know today. They command the respect of the American people, and they have our everlasting gratitude."

It is true, after all, that our veterans have not only guaranteed the peace in Europe for more than 60 years, but they have also preserved it for us here at home. And today, our "Total Force"—a name given for blending active and reserve military units into a cohesive whole—have a new assignment as part of a much bigger war on terrorism.

Our military forces are dealing with the global war on terrorism, as well as challenges in Iraq and elsewhere around the globe. They are engaged in a difficult struggle to make sure that Afghanistan and Iraq are never again a source of terror or a threat to the United States and our most prized assets—our freedom and our citizens. . . .

This generation of soldiers, sailors, airmen, marines, and coastguardsmen are making a real difference. They are changing the world for the better, exactly as America's military men and women have done for generations.

And I hope that none of us need be reminded that one day these men and women will take off their military uniforms and take up the honor of being called American veterans.

I also trust that none of us need be reminded that it is the veteran who defended our national security, who risked life and limb to serve thousands of miles away from loved ones, and who sacrificed daily to protect the lives of innocent men, women and children. . . .

Veterans Must Be Treated Well

At an earlier time in our history, our most revered Founding Father, George Washington, gave an eloquent warning, "The willingness with which our young people are likely to serve in any war, no matter how justified, shall be directly proportional to how they perceive the veterans of earlier wars were treated and appreciated by their nation."

In a more recent speech, President Ronald Reagan echoed the wisdom of our first president's remarks when in signing legislation that established the Department of Veterans Affairs [VA] he said, "America's debt to those who would fight for her defense doesn't end the day the uniform comes off. For the security of our nation, it must not end."

At a time when troops on the ground are protecting our security and defending our cherished freedoms, AMVETS is concerned that leaders in Congress are set to test the wisdom of these great leaders.

We are told, for instance, that the budget recommended by the administration and the majorities in the House and Senate is sufficient to care for sick and disabled veterans. We know it is not. We have experience in this regard.

As recently as last year [2004], AMVETS was told that the fiscal year 2005 budget approved by Congress was adequate. Simply stated: not true. If one asks VA, officials there will inform you that their equipment and maintenance accounts are being raided and transferred to health care operations accounts to help cover the current shortfall.

News reports make the same case. From across the country, reports provide clear evidence that VA is straining and failing to make ends meet.

Accounts of Financial Strain on VA

In Georgia, Augusta's veterans affairs medical center is looking at shortening the hours of its emergency facilities. The Augusta unit already sends trauma patients to the trauma unit at the Medical College of Georgia hospital, but administrators at the medical center say further changes must be made due to a lack of money, staff and existing resources.

In Colorado, the *Denver Post* reports that shortfalls in funding and staff have forced the Denver veterans' hospital to cut nearly 100 beds and reduce housekeeping to stretch limited funds. To save money, cleaning crews were directed to focus on patient areas and not to worry about offices and other parts of the hospital. Four years ago, the article states, federal inspectors found most areas of the hospital clean and adequately maintained. Recent inspections, however, find widespread filthy conditions. According to the *Post*, the current operating budget for the Denver facility is actually $700,000 less than that provided two years ago, despite increases in the costs of drugs, technology, staff and related medical inflation.

In Maine, the *Bangor Daily News* reports that the medical center at Togus is proposing some dramatic changes in mental health care, specialty medical services and medication coverage veterans receive. The report suggests switching veterans to less expensive medications and, in some cases, substituting different formulations altogether. Staffing changes also are proposed, including not filling existing vacancies and replacing pricey temporary staff with lower-paid, lesser-skilled employees. According to the hospital's documents, specialty services such as physical rehabilitation and audiology are already operating with fewer staff than needed, "resulting in long waiting lines, poor quality of service and poor customer satisfaction."

More Cuts in Services

In Michigan, a lack of funding is forcing clinics to stop taking new patients. Clinics in Oakland and Macomb counties as well as the main clinic in Detroit and the one in Pontiac have capped access, disallowing patients who seek basic medical services. The staff assistant to the director of John D. Dingell VA Medical Center in downtown Detroit said, "We're aware that it's an inconvenience for the veterans, but given our financial situation, we need to do some things to put a cap on our spending, and this is one of the ways of reducing our facility expenses."

In Pennsylvania, the *Altoona Mirror* reports that the [James E.] Van Zandt VA Medical Center will cut back on funding for patient services, eliminate money for military celebrations and strike all capital projects and hiring to erase a projected $5 million shortfall this year. The *Mirror* tells readers and veterans alike that at Van Zandt, treatment of patients and services provided will be decided on a "case-by-case basis." The report goes on to say that Van Zandt does not plan to add new jobs nor replace anyone who leaves a position at the center to help ends meet.

The Government Must Keep Veterans' Faith

It is the same story all across the country. Yet, we're told by administration spokespersons that this year's appropriation and next year's request will allow VA to continue providing of the highest quality of care for veterans.

AMVETS cannot believe that this astonishing situation is something the American people would support. We know that Americans are blessed to be citizens of this great nation, not just when times are good, but at all times. Together, we are part of something special, endowed by our creator in a great experiment to prove to the world that representative democracy is not only the most effective form of government, but also the only moral government. Generations of us have fought to build a better nation and we won't sit idly by and forget the debt we owe these heroic men and valiant women.

Veterans are told that VA health care costs too much. This is the reason that some in Congress have decided the lives and health of certain veterans do not matter. Frankly, that kind of thinking can get America into trouble. You cannot recruit future military if the word gets out that America does not keep the promises made to those who served her.

With troops on the ground defending American interests across the globe, keeping faith is not only the prudent thing to do; it's the right thing to do.

America Has an Obligation to Vets

Keeping faith with veterans requires that adequate resources be in place to provide for the benefits and services veterans earned through their military service. Attending to this obligation is one [of] the highest priorities in the nation. It ranks with our national defense and homeland security requirements.

The Office of Management and Budget and the Congressional Budget Office may not buy that story, and there may even be some folks on the Hill [Capitol Hill] that feel the same way. But the majority of Americans remain grateful and appreciative of the sacrifices veterans made for them. And they recognize that the expense of veterans' earned benefits is a cost of war.

The Effects of VA Funding Shortfalls

Across the country, VISNs [Veterans Integrated Service Networks] and hospitals are experiencing significant shortfalls. Their funding is both inadequate and unreliable. This flawed funding process produces many harmful effects:

- Denial of care to over 260,000 Priority 7 and 8 veterans

- Growing waiting lists, e.g., over 12,000 veterans were on VISN 16's electronic waiting list (EWL) for over 30 days in fall 2005

- Hiring freezes when facilities are facing hundreds of vacancies

- Pressure and/or requirement to work prolonged overtime

- Delayed facility construction and repairs, causing veterans to travel longer distances to get care

- Delays in equipment repair, requiring costly contracted services

- Closing of nursing units and other inpatient units

- Delayed CAT scans and MRIs, requiring costly outsourcing of tests

- Inability to staff new medical units

- Delays in surgery

American Federation of Government Employees,
"Budget Shortfalls and Outsourcing Remain Serious Threats
to VA Employees and Veterans," AFGE.org, September 29, 2006.

As for those who say veterans are clogging the VA health care system, no one at AMVETS would knowingly stand in the way of a disabled, sick military comrade seeking medical treatment at VA any more than they would deny being a citizen of this great country. We are American Veterans, and we are organized to help, not hinder.

In complete candor, I cannot tell you that in these past months, or under the present circumstances, we are comfortable with the direction taken by our congressional or executive leadership.

For instance, undersecretary of defense for personnel readiness David Chu told the *Wall Street Journal* that updated veteran and retiree benefits were damaging national security. Secretary Chu said that earned benefits "have gotten to where they are hurtful. They are taking away from the nation's ability to defend itself." . . . Chu's comments are hard to swallow. Simply stated, the brave men and women veterans of this great country are not the enemy of national security. . . .

AMVETS recognizes the VA health care system as the primary source of health care for our nation's veterans, especially those with service-connected injuries, those in need of specialized care and those who are indigent. It is a unique and irreplaceable national investment, critical to the nation and its veterans. In fact, many veterans consider access to high-quality health care to be one of their most important benefits.

Over the years, AMVETS has reported on chronic funding shortfalls that have resulted in denial, delay and rationing of veterans' health care. Our goal is to fund the Department of Veterans Affairs at levels necessary to allow the health care system to deliver the world-class services of which it is capable.

Restore Priority 8 Access

The members of AMVETS, however, remain deeply troubled by the current policy banning access to VA health care for certain veterans. Naturally, we continue, as always, to support generous assistance to those who have special needs arising from service in the armed forces, particularly combat service. We want to ensure that severely disabled veterans receive prompt care. But denying access only devalues the service of those who seek care with VA.

AMVETS would like to see VA begin the process of restoring Priority 8 [the lowest level on the VA's priority list] access, which could be started by enrolling those veterans who can identify their private- or public-health insurers and making certain that VA is eligible for medical reimbursement. The secretary has this discretionary authority under statute and, for our friends who hinge veterans' access to their ability to pay for it, this type of enrollment would ensure that third-party payers would be maximized to the fullest extent.

To augment direct appropriations, which are clearly needed, AMVETS also supports Medicare subvention as a way to enhance funding of VA health care. Medicare subvention could prove beneficial to veterans and the government. For veterans who have paid into Medicare throughout their working lives, VA subvention would mean greater access to care. And for the government, there would be savings, since nearly 60 percent of enrolled veterans are Medicare eligible and, according to VA, Medicare services can be delivered less expensively than in the private sector. . . . One of our greatest presidents once said, "It is common sense to take a method and try it. If it fails, admit it frankly and try another, but above all try something."

It is time to take President Franklin Delano Roosevelt's advice. It is time to try something different. AMVETS asks you to recognize that the current system of funding veterans health care is broken. It simply doesn't work. Too many sick and disabled veterans either cannot enroll in the system or wait too long for care.

AMVETS calls on Congress to replace the current discretionary funding process with assured funding for veterans health care. Assured funding of VA health care would provide a comprehensive solution to the current funding problem. Once health care funding matches the actual average cost of care for the veterans enrolled in the system, with annual indexing for inflation, VA can truly fulfill its mission.

"Inspired management has transformed the [Veterans Health Administration] . . . into a model organization that delivers higher quality health care than the average of private health care providers . . . at a comparatively reasonable price."

Assured Public Funding Is Not the Best Way to Fund VA Services

Henry J. Aaron

Henry J. Aaron is a senior fellow at the Brookings Institution, a nonpartisan public policy organization. In the following statement, he maintains that assured funding for the Department of Veterans Affairs (VA) is not the best option for managing VA funds. Aaron argues that assured funding will expand the VA, but it will not lead to reform of the VA health system, and it will likely boost federal spending.

As you read, consider the following questions:

1. How many hospitals, outpatient clinics, nursing homes, and rehabilitation centers does the VHA administer?

Henry J. Aaron, "Funding the U.S. Department of Veterans' Affairs of the Future," Statement Before the House Committee on Veterans' Affairs, Veterans Health Administration, October 3, 2007. Reproduced by permission of the author.

2. What kind of transformation has the VHA undergone since 1995?

3. Governments account for what percentage of national health care spending, according to Aaron?

In the course of my remarks, I should like to stress four points:

First, the VHA [Veterans Health Administration] faces an unusually difficult challenge—it must deliver an extraordinarily wide range of services to highly diverse populations. The VHA provides ordinary primary, secondary, and tertiary somatic medicine, as well as mental health services. One of its most important responsibilities is to offer a subtle combination of physical therapy, mental health services, and somatic treatment to victims of spinal cord and traumatic brain injury.

Second, the VHA has performed remarkably well of late. Inspired management has transformed the VHA from being the poster child for low-quality medical care into a model organization that delivers higher quality health care than the average of private health care providers and does so at a comparatively reasonable price.

Third, the budget of the VHA is part of the long roster of federally financed health care services. The cost of federal health care obligations is projected under current law to increase enormously. In fact, growth of these programs accounts for more than all of the long-term deficits recently to which the Congressional Budget Office [CBO] and various private analysts have recently drawn attention. Put more positively, if the nation deals with the imbalance between projected revenues and spending for health care, revenues at current levels are projected to be sufficient to pay for all other anticipated government commitments, including all Social Security benefits promised under current law.

Fourth, proposals to boost federal health care spending abound. Not all can be funded without unduly raising federal spending. Different groups would benefit from each of these proposed increases. Sensible budgeting requires a comparison of these competing claims. Unfortunately, congressional committee structure inhibits such comparisons. To illustrate this problem, I list three such candidates for increased spending. For what it is worth, my judgment is that the priority of converting VHA spending into mandatory [or assured] funding ranks below the other two possible uses of federal funds.

The VHA's Important Transformation

The VHA administers more than 1,200 hospitals, outpatient clinics, nursing homes, and rehabilitation facilities. These facilities comprise one of the largest health care delivery networks in the United States, with revenues approximating those of the largest private domestic health care system, Kaiser Permanente. . . .

America owes its thanks to all military veterans for their service to this nation. All took time from civilian lives to help protect the rest of us. But it in no way diminishes the contribution made by those veterans who came home healthy and uninjured and have prospered to say that the nation owes a special debt to those who suffer daily physical reminders of their service. . . .

The Veterans Health Administration has undergone a remarkable transformation since 1995. At the time, critics charged the VHA with high cost, low quality, providing the wrong mix of services for its clientele, and poor accessibility. The key reforms included reorganizing numerous separate providers into Veterans Integrated Service Networks (VISNs) that received budgets from which responsible officials had to manage [a] variety of service providers. Budget authority was shifted to where veterans were most numerous. These reforms gave the VHA authority to bargain over the prices of pharmaceutical products that, linked to the VHA's size, gives it more clout than virtually any other single purchaser. The performance of the VISNs is measured and advertised around the VHA and VISN managers [receiving] bonuses for good performance. These quite business-like incentives illustrate an important proposition: Government can achieve the efficiencies normally associated with private businesses if its managers are given the flexibility and incentives to operate effectively.

Unfortunately, Congress has interfered with the VHA's administrative freedoms in various ways and has made efficient administration more difficult than it needs to be. Congress has prevented the VHA from contracting with one or a few suppliers of some products whose prices are lowest. The late completion of work on budgets and the all-too-frequent use of continuing resolutions has hampered efficient hiring and other planning.

Electronic Medical Records

On a more positive note, the VHA has gone further and faster in introducing electronic medical records (EMRs) than have most private health care providers. EMRs could be introduced expeditiously because VHA management had centralized control, something that is lacking in nearly all of the private U.S. health care system. And it proceeded as fast as it did also because the VHA also had adequate financial backing—an estimated $300 million for wiring, $450 million for computers, and $485 million a year (an average of $90 per patient) in upkeep. The VHA experience illustrates why all the talk about electronic health records for the private sector has produced so few results. In contrast to the money that the VHA had to back its EMR "play," the legislation that created the Office of the National Coordinator for Health Information Technology stipulated that no additional funds would be appropriated to support its activities. One would be hard-pressed to find a better example of "you get what you pay for."

Objective measures indicate that the quality of care provided by the VHA at least equals that of private sector health services. One study that found that two-thirds of VA [Department of Veterans Affairs] patients but only 51 percent of privately served patients receive all indicated care when they see a doctor or visit a hospital. Another study reported that the VHA provided better care in twelve of thirteen categories than private providers rendered to Medicare patients.

These comparisons clearly indicate that the VHA has come a long way since the days when the quality of its care was almost universally criticized. They are also consistent with a view that, at least in the case of health care, a well-managed public agency, authorized by Congress to operate in a business-like manner, can deliver care as good as or better than that rendered by the private sector *as currently organized*. No doubt improvements in efficiency similar to those of the VHA could have been achieved in the private sector if current administrative arrangements were altered. Alas, the currently fragmented organization of private providers and payers alike deprives most of them of the capacity to execute the reforms that centralized management made possible in the VHA.

The Challenge of Providing Health Care

Governments—federal, state, and local—now directly account for 47 percent of national health care spending and an even larger share—56 percent—of hospital spending. The full role of governments is even larger than those numbers suggest, because premiums paid by employers for their employees are partially offset by the revenues forgone as a result of the exclusion of this portion of consumption from all tax, corporate or individual.

Although it is already large, the public share in the cost of health care is certain to increase. Growth of health care spending has outpaced the growth of income by an average of 2.7 percentage points a year for more than four decades. A gap of

The Projected Budget Deficit or Surplus

The Congressional Budget Office estimates a ballooning deficit in the next decades, unless one subtracts the rising spending on government healthcare programs Medicare and Medicaid.

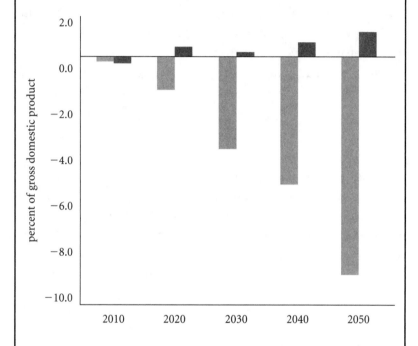

Projected deficit, excluding Medicare and Medicaid, and associated revenues
Projected deficit, including all expenditures (except interest) and revenues

TAKEN FROM: Henry J. Aaron, "Funding the U.S. Department of Veterans Affairs of the Future," Statement before the House Committee on Veterans Affairs, October 3, 2007.

similar size is likely to persist. The rate at which the menu of beneficial medical interventions increases is not expected to slow as the genomic revolution, nanotechnology, and personalized medicine proceed. Furthermore, the population is aging. The financial burden of supporting health care for the elderly disproportionately falls on the public. The proportion of the population covered by public programs will increase.

Furthermore, the value of the exclusion from tax of privately financed health insurance premiums will continue to grow faster than income does.

What is insufficiently understood, in my opinion, is that meeting this challenge will require a transformation of both publicly and privately financed health care. Measures to slow the growth of *both* public and private health care spending and to boost taxes will be necessary. This nation has come to a national consensus that Americans—old and young, with and without disabilities, rich and poor—should enjoy simi-lar—*not identical, but similar*—access to health care. Hospitals and physicians treat all patients similarly; indeed, if they do not, they are—and *should* be—open to successful suit for mal-practice. That the polity would long tolerate cuts in either Medicare or Medicaid sufficient to significantly lower the rate of growth of spending is, in my view, an insult to the generos-ity and compassion of the American people.

What is also inadequately understood is that successfully balancing public spending for and revenues dedicated to health care would eliminate any long-term budget problem, based on the best current projections. . . .

- The nation faces large long-term deficits under current policy.

- The nation does not face an overall fiscal crisis or an entitlement crisis: It faces a big health care financing problem that should lead to a vigorous national debate on [how] much health care we want and how to pay for it.

Is Assured or Mandatory Funding the Best Option?

Against this background, should funding for the VHA be con-verted from a discretionary to mandatory account? The an-swer, I believe, is that it should not, despite the genuine claim that veterans have on public support for their health care and the excellent record in delivery [of] high-quality health care at a reasonable price that the VHA has established in recent years.

- This switch would create incentives for undue expansion of the VHA.

- This expansion would very likely not be consistent with the longer term objectives of reforming the overall health care system.

- Finally, the conversion would likely boost federal spending at a time when other increases in federal health care spending would yield greater benefits.

At present, the VHA annually receives a fixed appropriation set by Congress based on the president's budget. If VHA funding were mandatory, it would presumably be based on actual enrollment multiplied by a sum set to approximate the per person cost of providing care to enrollees. This is the system proposed in [congressional bill] H.R. 2514. Baseline spending is to be set at a percentage of past spending—130 percent in H.R. 2514. Future funding would be based on baseline, per capita spending multiplied by enrollment in the VHA system in the preceding year multiplied by an index—the CPI [consumer price index] in H.R. 2514.

Increasing VHA Services

Such a system would likely create powerful incentives for the VHA to enroll as many veterans as possible, whether or not new enrollees use VHA services as much as current enrollees or even whether they use them at all. In fact, incentives would be strongest to enroll those expected *not* to use VHA services, as the resulting addition to budget would encourage VHA administrators to enhance services to entice others to join. As funding increases, the VHA would be able to enrich services, encouraging both current and new enrollees to increase the proportion of health care they seek from the VHA. The VHA now enrolls only about one-third and annually serves just over one-fifth of all veterans. Furthermore, nearly 80 percent have non-VHA health insurance coverage from public or private sources.

These facts mean that the potential for increasing VHA service levels is vast. The Congressional Budget Office, using similar reasoning, has estimated that converting the VHA to mandatory funding on the lines of the 2005 proposal would roughly double total spending. Some drop in spending under other government programs would occur, but, according to the Congressional Budget Office estimates of H.R. 515 submitted in 2005, which resembles H.R. 2514 submitted this year [2007], the offsets would be modest.

To be sure, converting the VHA to mandatory funding would not entirely insulate it from budgetary pressures. Congress could cut the per person funding amount or exclude certain groups of veterans from the formula used for computing annual funding. The funding formula contained in H.R. 2514 could be modified to hold down spending. But I think such modifications are unlikely to gain much traction.

Is an increase in VHA funding the best way to increase health care spending? Is it likely to move health care delivery in a direction that the nation is likely to follow? If the answers to these questions are "yes," then this budgetary commitment is justified. Each of us will have views on the answers to these questions. Mine is that the answers are "no."

VHA as Socialized Medicine

The VHA is the nearest approximation in the United States to the British National Health Service, a publicly funded entity that directly employs most health care providers. That form of organization differs from the U.S. norm—third-party payment to private hospitals, physicians, and other providers. It is unlikely to be widely adopted in the United States. Little support exists anywhere on the political spectrum for turning health care providers into public employees. All strategies for extending coverage—tax incentives, state initiatives, single payer, employer mandate, individual mandate—call for payments to private hospitals, physicians, and other providers. To encourage an increased fraction of the U.S. population to receive an increased proportion of its care from a system based on publicly employed and managed providers would be a step away from any future national system.

Furthermore, Congress is duty bound to weigh the relative merits of various proposals to boost public spending on health care. Such comparisons are difficult given the prevailing committee structure of the U.S. Congress, but it is right to make them.

- At present, Congress has just sent to the president [George W. Bush] a proposal to extend the State Children's Health Insurance Program [SCHIP], at an annual cost of approximately $7 billion over the next five years.

- Congress will likely prevent the full scheduled cut in physician reimbursement under Medicare from taking effect. CBO has estimated that the *cost of raising physician reimbursements 1 percentage point* instead of cutting them, as required under current law, would boost spending by an annual average of $4.8–$6 billion over the next five years [2008–2012].

- I have not seen a cost estimate for H.R. 2514. Adjusting the estimate for H.R. 515 for the passage of time and the change of index for per-person costs, leads to an estimate of increased annual outlay of $45–50 billion over the next five years.

The current budgetary climate will not readily accommodate spending increases that boost the budget deficit. Indeed, part of the controversy surrounding SCHIP is its cost, despite the fact that it would be offset by increased tobacco taxes. Furthermore, making VHA funding mandatory would not be offset by reduced spending elsewhere or by increased revenues. It is not yet clear whether any added spending to avoid reductions in physician reimbursements under Medicare will be offset. But what is clear is that the deficit increasing effect of H.R. 2514 is vastly larger than that of either of the other two bills.

On substantive grounds, and contrary to allegations of some of its critics, the SCHIP bill builds on and reinforces the private provision of health care. SCHIP has enjoyed bipartisan support since its enactment in 1997. Avoiding the full reduction in physician reimbursements under Medicare is necessary in order to discourage significant and possibly catastrophic defections by physicians from being participating providers or even participating in the Medicare program at all. Both uses of public funds reinforce established ways of providing health care to dependent populations, building on a public-private partnership. Both these measures should enjoy far higher priority than does H.R. 2514.

"If Congress does decide to expand benefits to non-service-related conditions and lower-priority veterans, then it should consider alternatives to expanding the existing VA medical system."

VA Health Care Is Not a Flexible System and Should Not Be Expanded

Nina Owcharenko

Nina Owcharenko is a senior policy analyst in the Center for Health Policy Studies at the Heritage Foundation, a conservative public policy think tank. In the following viewpoint, she argues that if the U.S. government wants to provide health care services to more veterans, the solution is not to expand the size and scope of the medical system of the Department of Veterans Affairs (VA). Instead, policy makers should consider alternative solutions, such as authorizing health insurance subsidies for eligible veterans.

As you read, consider the following questions:

1. How does the VA categorize veterans in their health care system?

Nina Owcharenko, "Proceed with Caution: The Unintended Consequences of Expanding VA Access," Web Memo, Heritage Foundation, March 17, 2006. Copyright © 2006 The Heritage Foundation. Reproduced by permission.

2. Why does the author feel that spreading VA resources across a broader population is a bad choice?

3. Why does the author believe that the subsidy program is a better option than expanding VA health care?

To provide improved health care services to more veterans, some propose to expand the size and scope of the [Department of] Veterans Affairs (VA) medical system beyond its current population and capacity. The core mission of the VA is "to serve current combat veterans and veterans with service disabilities, lower incomes, and special needs." Efforts to broaden this mission to include nearly all veterans are unwise. Rather than expand the VA's role, policy makers should consider alternatives that would preserve the core mission of the VA medical system while providing more meaningful assistance to others who have served the United States.

The VA's Unique Structure

Unlike Medicare and Medicaid, which reimburse private providers, the VA medical system is owned and operated by the VA. The VA builds its own hospitals and facilities and hires its own physicians and ancillary health care providers as employees. The VA does have some advantages. For example, the VA has a long tradition of training medical students and recently has implemented a state-of-the-art information technology (IT) system to improve patient care.

The VA currently receives its funding at Congress's discretion. Because these funds are limited, Congress required the VA to categorize each veteran into one of seven classes, from the highest priority (Priority 1) to lowest (Priority 7). In 2002, Congress created Priority 8, separating higher-income veterans suffering from conditions not related to their service from Priority 7, thus, reserving Priority 7 for lower-income veterans suffering from such conditions. In 2003, the [George W.] Bush

© 2008 Paresh Nath, The *National Herald*, India and PoliticalCartoons.com.

administration suspended new enrollment of Priority 8 veterans so that the VA could focus on those veterans most in need.

Unintended Consequences

As with any government-run health care program, the VA's greatest difficulty is balancing cost and demand. Health care costs have been rising across the economy, and the VA program is no exception. In 2001, the VA spent $21 billion on medical care for veterans. In 2004, this spending reached $27 billion, and it is expected to reach $30 billion by 2007. Between 2001 and 2004, the number of patients treated in the VA system increased 22 percent from 4 million in 2001 to 5 million. Of the veterans currently enrolled in the VA [as of 2006], only 27 percent are in the lower-priority categories.

While the VA provides high-quality care to the veterans that it serves, forcing the VA to spread its limited resources across a broader, more diverse population could put the quality of care for the most needy and deserving at risk. The VA is known for its specialized treatments and for dealing with difficult and complex health conditions. Expanding its services to meet the basic health care needs of the broader veteran population could cause general health services to crowd out more specialized treatment within the system.

Incorporating a large pool of new beneficiaries with less-specialized medical needs into the system would alter the political and budget calculus of the VA system. Because beneficiaries with general needs would substantially outnumber beneficiaries with specialized needs, future attempts to control cost growth would likely restrict access to specialized care.

The experience of Medicaid, the government health care program for the poor, demonstrates the danger of expanding a health care program beyond its original purpose. The more Medicaid eligibility expands up the income scale, the more cost-containment measures are imposed to keep expenditures under control. However, many of these techniques actually put patients at greater risk. For example, limitations on prescription drug access in Medicaid have had significant adverse effects on some of the most vulnerable populations, such as the mentally disabled. In the VA system, the most vulnerable would be those veterans injured in service to their country.

A Better Solution

Congress should recognize that two separate issues are at play in this debate. The first is whether additional health care benefits should be provided to all veterans, and the second is how such additional benefits might be provided. If Congress does decide to expand benefits to non-service-related conditions and lower-priority veterans, then it should consider alternatives to expanding the existing VA medical system.

For example, Congress could authorize and fund health insurance subsidies for certain lower-priority categories of veterans that would assist them in purchasing private health insurance coverage and related medical services. Because these veterans suffer from conditions that are indistinguishable from those suffered in the general population, the same arrangements that cover the general population are well designed to cover them. A subsidy program would allow the VA to continue to focus on those who are in most need while providing some assistance to more of those who served their country.

Two advantages of this approach are particularly important. First, subsidies would ensure continuity of coverage and care for the vast majority of veterans in the lower-priority categories who already have insurance coverage and relationships with hospitals and doctors. Second, it would avoid the substantial capital expenditures necessary to expand the current VA system to accommodate more patients.

In terms of both total cost and quality of care for all veterans, expanding the VA medical system is not the best way to provide improved health care services to those veterans now outside of the system. Subsidies to purchase private insurance plans would serve these veterans better and protect the care that those who were injured in service to their country depend upon.

> "Because the [Veterans Health Administration] is a big, government-run system that has nearly a lifetime relationship with its patients, it has incentives for investing in quality and keeping its patients well."

The VHA Could Be the Model for Future Health Care

Phillip Longman

Phillip Longman is a Schwartz Senior Fellow at the New America Foundation. In the following viewpoint, he notes that the impressive turnaround of the health care system of the Department of Veterans Affairs (VA) can provide a blueprint for reforming America's health care system. Longman discusses the lessons to be found in the VA system—including improved cost and quality of care—and their applicability for the larger population.

As you read, consider the following questions:

1. According to an independent survey, what percentage of Veterans Health Administration (VHA) hospital patients express satisfaction with the care they receive?

Phillip Longman, "The Best Care Anywhere," *Washington Monthly*, January–February 2005. Copyright © 2005 by Washington Monthly Publishing, LLC, 733 15th St. NW, Suite 520, Washington DC 20005. (202) 393-5155. Web site: www.washingtonmonthly .com. Reproduced by permission.

2. What percentage of Medicare and Medicaid patients express satisfaction with the care they receive?

3. What did Kenneth W. Kizer do to reform the VHA system?

Quick. When you read "veterans hospital," what comes to mind? Maybe you recall the headlines from a dozen years ago about the three decomposed bodies found near a veterans medical center in Salem, Virginia. Two turned out to be the remains of patients who had wandered months before. The other body had been resting in place for more than 15 years. The Veterans Health Administration (VHA) admitted that its search for the missing patients had been "cursory."

Or maybe you recall images from movies like *Born on the Fourth of July*, in which Tom Cruise plays a wounded Vietnam vet who becomes radicalized by his shabby treatment in a crumbling, rat-infested veterans hospital in the Bronx. Sample dialogue: "This place is a [f---in'] slum!"

By the mid-1990s, the reputation of veterans hospitals had sunk so low that conservatives routinely used their example as a kind of reductio ad absurdum critique of any move toward "socialized medicine." Here, for instance, is Jarret B. Wollstein, a right-wing activist/author, railing against the [former president Bill] Clinton health care plan in 1994: "To see the future of health care in America for you and your children under Clinton's plan," Wollstein warned, "just visit any Veterans Administration [currently the Department of Veterans Affairs (VA)] hospital. You'll find filthy conditions, shortages of everything, and treatment bordering on barbarism."

And so it goes today. If the debate is over health care reform, it won't be long before some free-market conservative will jump up and say that the sorry shape of the nation's veterans hospitals just proves what happens when government gets into the health care business. And if he's a true believer, he'll then probably go on to suggest, quoting William Safire [a political columnist] and other free marketers, that the government should just shut down the whole miserable system and provide veterans with health care vouchers.

The Surprising Quality of VHA Hospitals

Yet here's a curious fact that few conservatives or liberals know. Who do you think receives higher quality health care. Medicare patients who are free to pick their own doctors and specialists? Or aging veterans stuck in those presumably filthy VA hospitals with their antiquated equipment, uncaring administrators, and incompetent staff? An answer came in 2003, when the prestigious *New England Journal of Medicine* published a study that compared veterans health facilities on 11 measures of quality with fee-for-service Medicare. On all 11 measures, the quality of care in veterans facilities proved to be "significantly better."

Here's another curious fact. The *Annals of Internal Medicine* recently published a study that compared veterans health facilities with commercial managed care systems in their treatment of diabetes patients. In seven out of seven measures of quality, the VA provided better care.

It gets stranger. Pushed by large employers who are eager to know what they are buying when they purchase health care for their employees, an outfit called the National Committee for Quality Assurance [NCQA] today ranks health care plans on 17 different performance measures. These include how well the plans manage high blood pressure or how precisely they adhere to standard protocols of evidence-based medicine such as prescribing beta blockers for patients recovering from a heart attack. Winning NCQA's seal of approval is the gold standard in the health care industry. And who do you suppose this year's winner is: Johns Hopkins [Hospital]? Mayo Clinic? Massachusetts General [Hospital]? Nope. In every single category, the VHA system outperforms the highest rated non-VHA hospital.

Veterans Love VA Health Care

Not convinced? Consider what vets themselves think. Sure, it's not hard to find vets who complain about difficulties in establishing eligibility. Many are outraged that the [George W.] Bush administration has decided to deny previously promised health care benefits to veterans who don't have service-related illnesses or who can't meet a strict means test. Yet these grievances are about access to the system, not about the quality of care received by those who get in. Veterans groups tenaciously defend the VHA and applaud its turnaround. "The quality of care is outstanding," says Peter Gayton, deputy director for veterans affairs and rehabilitation at the American Legion. In the latest independent survey, 81 percent of VHA hospital patients express satisfaction with the care they receive, compared to 77 percent of Medicare and Medicaid patients.

Outside experts agree that the VHA has become an industry leader in its safety and quality measures. Dr. Donald M. Berwick, president of the Institute for Healthcare Improvement and one of the nation's top health care quality experts, praises the VHA's information technology as "spectacular." The venerable Institute of Medicine notes that the VHA's "integrated health information system, including its framework for using performance measures to improve quality, is considered one of the best in the nation."

If this gives you cognitive dissonance, it should. The story of how and why the VHA became the benchmark for quality medicine in the United States suggests that much of what we think we know about health care and medical economics is just wrong. It's natural to believe that more competition and consumer choice in health care would lead to greater quality and lower costs, because in almost every other realm, it does. That's why the Bush administration—which has been promoting greater use of information technology and other quality improvement in health care—also wants to give individuals new tax-free "health savings accounts" and high-deductible insurance plans. Together, these measures are supposed to encourage patients to do more comparison shopping and haggling with their doctors; therefore, they create more market discipline in the system.

But when it comes to health care, it's a government bureaucracy that's setting the standard for maintaining best practices while reducing costs, and it's the private sector that's lagging in quality. That unexpected reality needs examining if we're to have any hope of understanding what's wrong with America's health care system and how to fix it. It turns out that precisely because the VHA is a big, government-run system that has nearly a lifetime relationship with its patients, it has incentives for investing in quality and keeping its patients well—incentives that are lacking in for-profit medicine.

Hitting Bottom

By the mid-1990s, the veterans health care system was in deep crisis. A quarter of its hospital beds were empty. Government audits showed that many VHA surgeons had gone a year without picking up a scalpel. The population of veterans was falling sharply, as aging World War II and Korean War vets began to pass away. At the same time, a mass migration of veterans from the Snowbelt to the Sunbelt overwhelmed hospitals in places such as Tampa with new patients, while those in places such as Pittsburgh had wards of empty beds.

Serious voices called for simply dismantling the VA system. Richard Kogan, a senior fellow at the Center on Budget and Policy Priorities in Washington, told the New York Times in 1994: "The real question is whether there should be a veterans health care system at all." At a time when the other health care systems were expanding outpatient clinics, the VHA still required hospital stays for routine operations like cataract surgery. A patient couldn't even receive a pair of crutches without checking in. Its management system was so ossified and top-down that permission for such trivial expenditures as

$9.82 for a computer cable had to be approved in Washington at the highest levels of the bureaucracy.

Yet few politicians dared to go up against the powerful veterans lobby, or against the many unions that represented much of the VHA's workforce. Instead, members of Congress fought to have new veterans hospitals built in their districts, or to keep old ones from being shuttered. Three weeks before the 1996 presidential election, in part to keep pace with [Republican candidate] Bob Dole's promises to veterans, President Clinton signed a bill that planned, as he put it, to "furnish comprehensive medical services to all veterans," regardless of their income or whether they had service-related disabilities.

Reforming the System

So, it may have been politics as usual that kept the floundering veterans health care system going. Yet behind the scenes, a few key players within the VHA had begun to look at ways in which the system might heal itself. Chief among them was Kenneth W. Kizer, who in 1994 had become VHA's undersecretary for health, or, in effect, the system's CEO [chief executive officer].

A physician trained in emergency medicine and public health, Kizer was an outsider who immediately started upending the VHA's entrenched bureaucracy. He oversaw a radical downsizing and decentralization of management power, implemented pay-for-performance contracts with top executives, and won the right to fire incompetent doctors. He and his team also began to transform the VHA from an acute care, hospital-based system into one that put far more resources into primary care and outpatient services for the growing number of aging veterans beset by chronic conditions.

By 1998, Kizer's shake-up of the VHA's operating system was already earning him management guru status in an era in which management gurus were practically demigods. His story appeared that year in a book titled *Straight from the CEO: The World's Top Business Leaders Reveal Ideas That Every Manager Can Use* published by Price Waterhouse and Simon & Schuster. Yet the most dramatic transformation of the VHA didn't just involve such trendy, 1990's ideas as downsizing and reengineering. It also involved an obsession with systematically improving quality and safety that to this day is still largely lacking throughout the rest of the private health care system. . . .

Health for Service

Consider why, ultimately, the veterans health system is such an outlier in its commitment to quality. Partly it's because of timely, charismatic leadership. A quasi-military culture may also facilitate acceptance of new technologies and protocols. But there are also other important, underlying factors.

First, unlike virtually all other health care systems in the United States, VHA has a near lifetime relationship with its patients. Its customers don't jump from one health plan to the next every few years. They start a relationship with the VHA as early as their teens, and it endures. That means that the VHA actually has an incentive to invest in prevention and more effective disease management. When it does so, it isn't just saving money for somebody else. It's maximizing its own resources.

The system's doctors are salaried, which also makes a difference. Most could make more money doing something else, so their commitment to their profession most often derives from a higher-than-usual dose of idealism. Moreover, because they are not profit maximizers, they have no need to be fearful of new technologies or new protocols that keep people well. Nor do they have an incentive to clamor for high-tech devices that don't improve the system's quality or effectiveness of care.

And, because it is a well-defined system, the VHA can act like one. It can systematically attack patient safety issues. It

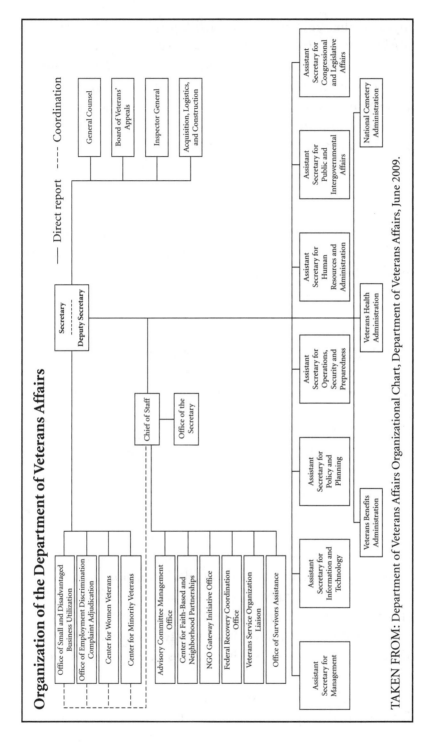

Organization of the Department of Veterans Affairs

— Direct report ---- Coordination

Secretary
Deputy Secretary

General Counsel

Board of Veterans' Appeals

Inspector General

Acquisition, Logistics, and Construction

Chief of Staff

Office of the Secretary

Office of Small and Disadvantaged Business Utilization

Office of Employment Discrimination Complaint Adjudication

Center for Women Veterans

Center for Minority Veterans

Advisory Committee Management Office

Center for Faith-Based and Neighborhood Partnerships

NGO Gateway Initiative Office

Federal Recovery Coordination Office

Veterans Service Organization Liaison

Office of Survivors Assistance

Assistant Secretary for Management

Assistant Secretary for Information and Technology

Assistant Secretary for Policy and Planning

Assistant Secretary for Operations, Security and Preparedness

Assistant Secretary for Human Resources and Administration

Assistant Secretary for Public and Intergovernmental Affairs

Assistant Secretary for Congressional and Legislative Affairs

Veterans Benefits Administration

Veterans Health Administration

National Cemetery Administration

TAKEN FROM: Department of Veterans Affairs Organizational Chart, Department of Veterans Affairs, June 2009.

can systematically manage information using standard platforms and interfaces. It can systematically develop and implement evidence-based standards of care. It can systematically discover where its care needs improvement and take corrective measures. In short, it can do what the rest of the health care sector can't seem to, which is to pursue quality systematically without threatening its own financial viability.

Hmm. That gives me an idea. No one knows how we're ever going to provide health care for all these aging baby boomers. Meanwhile, in the absence of any near-term major wars, the population of veterans in the United States will fall dramatically in the next decade. Instead of shuttering underutilized VHA facilities, maybe we should build more. What if we expanded the veterans health care system and allowed anyone who is either already a vet or who agrees to perform two years of community service a chance to buy in? Indeed, what if we said to young and middle-aged people, if you serve your community and your country, you can make your parents or other loved ones eligible for care in an expanded VHA system?

VA Health Care System Should Be a Model

The system runs circles around Medicare in both cost and quality. Unlike Medicare, it's allowed by law to negotiate for deep drug discounts, and does. Unlike Medicare, it provides long-term nursing home care. And it demonstrably delivers some of the best, if not the best, quality health care in the United States with amazing efficiency. Between 1999 and 2003, the number of patients enrolled in the VHA system increased by 70 percent, yet funding (not adjusted for inflation) increased by only 41 percent. So the VHA has not only become the health care industry's best quality performer, it has done so while spending less and less on each patient. Decreasing cost and improving quality go hand in hand in industries like autos and computers—but in health care, such a relationship

[is] virtually unheard of. The more people we can get into the VHA, the more efficient and effective the American health care system will be. . . .

Once fully implemented, the plan would allow Americans to avoid skipping from one health care plan to the next over their lifetimes, with all the discontinuities in care and record keeping and disincentives to preventative care that this entails. No matter where you moved in the country, or how often you changed jobs, or where you might happen to come down with an illness, there would be a VHA facility nearby where your complete medical records would be available and the same evidence-based protocols of medicine would be practiced.

Consumers Should Have a Choice

You might decide that such a plan is not for you. But, as with mass transit, an expanded VHA would offer you a benefit even if you didn't choose to use it. Just as more people riding commuter trains means fewer cars in your way, more people using the VHA would mean less crowding in your own, private doctor's waiting room, as well as more pressure on your private health care network to match the VHA's performance on cost and quality.

Why make public service a requirement for receiving VHA care? Because it's in the spirit of what the veterans health care system is all about. It's not an entitlement; it's recognition for those who serve. America may not need as many soldiers as in the past, but it has more need than ever for people who will volunteer to better their communities.

Would such a system stand in danger of becoming woefully underfunded, just as the current VHA system is today? Veterans comprise a declining share of the population, and the number of Americans who have personal contact with military life continues to shrink. It is therefore not surprising that veterans health care issues barely register on the national agenda, even in times of war. But, as with any government benefit, the broader the eligibility, the more political support it is likely to receive. Many veterans will object to the idea of sharing their health care system with non-vets; indeed, many already have issues with the VHA treating vets who do not have combat-related disabilities. But in the long run, extending eligibility to non-vets may be the only way to ensure that more veterans get the care they were promised and deserve.

Does this plan seem too radical? Well, perhaps it does for now. We'll have to let the ranks of the uninsured further swell, let health care costs consume larger and larger portions of payrolls and household budgets, let more and more Americans die from medical errors and mismanaged care, before any true reform of the health care system becomes possible. But it is time that our debates over health care took the example of the veterans health care system into account and tried to learn some lessons from it.

> *"Education is the currency that can purchase success in the 21st century, and this is the opportunity that our troops have earned."*

The United States Needs an Advanced GI Bill

Barack Obama

Barack Obama is the forty-fourth president of the United States. In the following viewpoint, he praises the valuable contribution of U.S. veterans and asserts that a new GI bill—which will provide financial support for education to those who served in the military after the terrorist attacks of September 11, 2001—is not only a recognition of and payback for those contributions, but also an investment in the future of the United States.

As you read, consider the following questions:

1. What did President Franklin Delano Roosevelt say about the veterans of World War II?

2. What percentage of college students were U.S. veterans by the year 1947?

3. How many Americans were educated as a result of the original GI Bill?

Barack Obama, "Remarks by the President on the Post-9/11 GI Bill," WhiteHouse.gov, August 3, 2009.

I'm honored to . . . renew our commitment to ensure that the men and women who wear the uniform of the United States of America get the opportunities that they have earned. I was a proud co-sponsor of the Post-9/11 GI Bill [the Post-9/11 Veterans Educational Assistance Act, which provides financial support for education to those who served in the military after the terrorist attacks of September 11, 2001] as senator. I'm committed to working with Secretary [of the Department of Veterans Affairs Eric K.] Shinseki to see that it is successfully implemented as president.

Why a New GI Bill?

And we do this not just to meet our moral obligation to those who've sacrificed greatly on our behalf and on behalf of the country. We do it because these men and women must now be prepared to lead our nation in the peaceful pursuit of economic leadership in the 21st century.

This generation of servicemen and women has already earned a place of honor in American history. Each of them signed up to serve, many after they knew that they would be sent into harm's way. Over the last eight years [2001–2009], they have endured tour after tour of duty in dangerous and distant places. They've experienced grueling combat—from the streets of Fallujah to the harsh terrain of Helmand province. They've adapted to complex insurgencies, protected local populations, and trained foreign security forces. So by any measure, they are the authors of one of the most extraordinary chapters of military service in the history of our nation.

And I don't make that statement lightly. For we know that anyone who puts on the uniform joins an unbroken line of selfless patriots that stretches back to Lexington and Concord [in the American Revolutionary War in 1775]. The freedom and prosperity that we enjoy would not exist without the service of generations of Americans who were willing to bear the heaviest and most dangerous burden.

But we also know this: The contributions that our servicemen and women can make to this nation do not end when they take off that uniform. We owe a debt to all who serve. And when we repay that debt to those bravest Americans among us, then we are investing in our future—not just their future, but also the future of our own country.

Historical Context

Now, this was the lesson that America was sometimes too slow to learn. After the Civil War and World War I, we saw far too many veterans who were denied the chance to live their dreams—men who were unable to find in peace the hope that they had fought for in war.

And FDR [former president Franklin Delano Roosevelt] knew this. In 1943, before the beaches of Normandy were stormed and the treacherous terrain of Iwo Jima was taken, he told the nation that the veterans of World War II would be treated differently. He said that they must not be demobilized, and I quote, "to a place on a bread line"—demobilized "to a place on a bread line or on a corner selling apples." Instead, Roosevelt said, "The American people will insist on fulfilling this American obligation to the men and women in the armed forces who are winning this war for us."

That is precisely what the American people did. The GI Bill [Servicemen's Readjustment Act] was approved just weeks after D-Day [June 6, 1944], and carried with it a simple promise to all who had served: You pick the school, we'll help pick up the bill. And what followed was not simply an opportunity for our veterans—it was a transformation for our country. By 1947, half of all Americans enrolled in college were veterans. Ultimately, this would lead to three presidents, three Supreme Court justices, 14 Nobel Prize winners, and two dozen Pulitzer Prize winners. But more importantly, it produced hundreds of thousands of scientists and engineers, doctors and nurses—the backbone of the largest middle class in history. All told, nearly 8 million Americans were educated under the original GI Bill, including my grandfather.

The Impact of the GI Bill

No number can sum up this sea change in our society. Reginald Wilson, a fighter pilot from Detroit, said, "I didn't know anyone who went to college. I never would have gone to college had it not been for the GI Bill." H.G. Jones, a Navy man from North Carolina, said, "What happened in my rural Caswell County community happened all over the country—going to college was no longer a novelty." Indeed, one of the men who went to college on the GI Bill, as I mentioned, was my grandfather, and I would not be standing here today if that opportunity had not led him West in search of opportunity.

So we owe the same obligations to this generation of servicemen and women, as was afforded that previous generation. That is the promise of the Post-9/11 GI Bill. It's driven by the same simple logic that drove the first GI Bill—you pick the school, we'll help pick up the bill. And looking out at the audience today, I'm proud to see so many veterans who will be able to pursue their education with this new support from the American people.

And this is even more important than it was in 1944. The GI Bill helped build a post-war economy that has been transformed by revolutions in communications and technology. And that's why the Post-9/11 GI Bill must give today's veterans the skills and training they need to fill the jobs of tomorrow. Education is the currency that can purchase success in the 21st century, and this is the opportunity that our troops have earned.

I'm also proud that all who have borne the burden of service these last several years will have access to this opportu-

The Post-9/11 GI Bill and Its Benefits

Individuals serving an aggregate period of active duty after September 10, 2001, of:	Includes entry level and skill training?	Percentage of Maximum Benefit
At least 36 months	Yes	100
At least 30 continuous days on active duty (Discharged due to service-connected disability)	Yes	100
At least 30 months, but less than 36 months	Yes	90
At least 24 months, but less than 30 months	Yes	80
At least 18 months, but less than 24 months	No	70
At least 12 months, but less than 18 months	No	60
At least 06 months, but less than 12 months	No	50
At least 90 days, but less than 06 months	No	40

TAKEN FROM: Veterans Outreach Letter, Department of Veterans Affairs, 2009.

nity. We are including Reservists and National Guard members, because they have carried out unprecedented deployments in Afghanistan and Iraq. We are including the military families who have sacrificed so much, by allowing the transfer of unused benefits to family members. And we are including those who pay the ultimate price by making this benefit available to the children of those who lost their lives in service to their country.

The GI Bill Is an Investment in the Future of America

This is not simply a debt that we are repaying to the remarkable men and women who have served—it is an investment in our own country. The first GI Bill paid for itself many times over through the increased revenue that came from a generation of men and women who received the skills and education that they needed to create their own wealth. The veterans who are here today—like the young post-9/11 veterans around the country—can lead the way to a lasting economic recovery and become the glue that holds our communities together. They, too, can become the backbone of a growing American middle class.

And even as we help our veterans learn the skills they need to succeed, I know that all of us can learn something from the men and women who serve our country. We have lived through an age when many people and institutions have acted irresponsibly—when service often took a backseat to short-term profits; when hard choices were put aside for somebody else, for some other time. It's a time when easy distractions became the norm, and the trivial has been taken too seriously.

The men and women who have served since 9/11 tell us a different story. While so many were reaching for the quick buck, they were heading out on patrol. While our discourse often produced more heat than light, especially here in Washington [D.C.], they have put their very lives on the line for America. They have borne the responsibility of war. And now, with this policy, we are making it clear that the United States of America must reward responsibility, and not irresponsibility. Now, with this policy, we are letting those who have borne the heaviest burden lead us into the 21st century.

And so today, we honor the service of an extraordinary generation, and look to an America that they will help build tomorrow. With the Post-9/11 GI Bill, we can give our veterans the chance to live their dreams. And we can help unleash their talents and tap their creativity and be guided by their sense of responsibility to their fellow citizens and to this country that we all love so much.

> *"The GI Bill was perfect for its time, but that doesn't make it perfect for ours."*

The United States Does Not Need an Advanced GI Bill

Steve Chapman

Steve Chapman is a columnist for the Chicago Tribune. *In the following viewpoint, he argues that a new GI bill is not the best way to reward veterans for their service, contending that the existing educational benefits and compensation for veterans are adequate. Chapman also predicts that by passing a new GI bill, reenlistment rates for the military will drop as soldiers will leave the service to take advantage of improved educational opportunities.*

As you read, consider the following questions:

1. How were veterans of World War I treated, according to Chapman?

2. Why does the author believe that the U.S. government doesn't need to further compensate veterans?

3. What kind of educational benefits already exist for veterans, according to the viewpoint?

When American soldiers returned from World War II, the nation thanked them with the GI Bill [Servicemen's Readjustment Act], which allowed millions of people to go to college at government expense. Sen. [Senator] Jim Webb, D-Va., thinks if it was good enough for the Greatest Generation [those Americans who grew up in the Great Depression and fought in World War II], it's good enough for this one. He wants to enact a new version of that program—an idea that may appeal to the heart but should give pause to the head.

The GI Bill, enacted in 1944, was an exceptional undertaking. It opened up higher education to a lot of people who would never have gone to college without it, transforming American society.

Good Reasons for the First GI Bill

It is now remembered as the visionary product of a nation's gratitude. In reality, the motives were more complicated than that. No one wanted to repeat the experience of World War I, when, as the Department of Veterans Affairs [VA] reports, "discharged veterans got little more than a $60 allowance and a train ticket home"—and later, embittered, marched on Washington [D.C.] to demand their due.

With the Great Depression still fresh in memory, President Franklin [Delano] Roosevelt's administration was also terrified that hordes of veterans would flood the job market and find no jobs. Sending them to college was seen as a way to avert mass unemployment.

A New GI Bill Is Not Needed

Those factors are not the only major justifications that are absent today. World War II was fought mostly by draftees, who were paid a pittance and kept at the front for as long as Uncle Sam needed them. Today's military consists entirely of volunteers, who signed up knowing that enlistment might mean long combat tours.

© 2009 Keefe, The *Denver Post* and PoliticalCartoons.com.

Military pay has vastly improved since D-Day [June 6, 1944]. A modern private gets the equivalent of double the salary paid back then, plus benefits that were not available to Private Ryan [referring to a World War II movie character].

The original GI bill was a way of compensating veterans who had been poorly compensated while in uniform. Our all-volunteer force, by contrast, pays competitive salaries, because it has to, and the competition is particularly keen at the moment. Bonuses for army enlistment now average $16,500 and go as high as $40,000—money that can be put away for school.

That's on top of existing educational benefits. The current GI bill offers some $38,000 for college. Additional aid is available through programs like the Army College Fund, which can nearly double that amount.

A GI Bill Is Not the Best Assistance for Veterans

Webb, a Marine Corps veteran, thinks more is in order. His proposal would cover four years of full tuition at the most expensive public institution in the state where the veteran en-

223

rolls, plus books, fees and $1,000 a month for living expenses. We owe this much, he says, to "our heroic veterans who have sacrificed so much for our great nation."

He has a point. Given the exceptional and unforeseen demands placed on today's regular military and reserves, there is nothing wrong with the nation deciding to thank the troops in a tangible way. But expanded college assistance isn't necessarily the best expression of gratitude.

In the first place, some people don't want to pursue higher education, and Webb's bill would leave them out in the cold. If we want to thank all our men and women in uniform, cash would be a better option. Some veterans could use the money to go to school, but others could use it to start a business or buy a home.

The New GI Bill Will Hurt the Military

In the second place, enriching educational benefits has a definite downside: It would complicate the task of keeping our overstretched military at full strength. John Warner, an economist at Clemson University who has studied the issue for the Pentagon, says additional aid could attract more recruits who want to go to college—but could also stimulate those in uniform to pass up reenlistment to pursue their education.

If the Webb program became law, Warner says, reenlistment rates could drop by 5 to 10 percentage points. And some of those hitting the exits would take valuable skills that are hard to replace. Given the intense strains on the military, this is no time to be enticing its best soldiers to leave.

At the end of World War II, keeping people from leaving the military was the least of our problems. President Roosevelt and the 78th Congress tailored their efforts to the unique challenges they faced. The GI Bill was perfect for its time, but that doesn't make it perfect for ours.

Periodical Bibliography

The following articles have been selected to supplement the diverse views presented in this chapter.

David Botti — "Trying to Modernize the GI Bill," *Newsweek*, April 29, 2008.

Megan Eckstein — "Colleges Cite Inequities in New Benefits for Veterans," *Chronicle of Higher Education*, April 17, 2009.

Kelly Field — "Veterans Affairs Department Cancels Plan to Outsource New Education Benefit," *Chronicle of Higher Education*, November 6, 2008.

Kristin M. Hall — "Colleges Focus on Veterans as GI Bill Ups Numbers," ABC News, July 5, 2009.

Douglas Herrmann, Douglas Raybeck, and Roland Wilson — "College Is for Veterans, Too," *Chronicle of Higher Education*, November 21, 2008.

Pamela Passman — "Let's Bridge the Gap for Vets Returning to the Private Sector," Politico.com, March 8, 2010. www.politico.com.

Paul Rieckhoff — "GI Bill 2010: A Quick Update," *Huffington Post*, March 4, 2010.

Jack Stripling — "Pat Tillman's Legacy: More Help for Military Veterans in College," *USA Today*, March 12, 2010.

Thom Wilborn — "VA Funding Reform: History in the Making," *DAV Magazine*, January–February 2010.

For Further Discussion

Chapter 1

1. Is enough being done to help U.S. military veterans? Review the viewpoints by Judith Coburn and Eric K. Shinseki to inform your opinion.

2. In his viewpoint, Ben Shapiro argues that recent portrayals of U.S. military vets are too negative. Tara McKelvey contends that such portrayals reflect true and complex experiences of many veterans. How do you think film writers and directors might go about researching roles portraying veterans in order to present them in fair and balanced ways?

3. Mental health outreach is an important aspect of providing mental health care to veterans. After reading viewpoints by Reynaldo Leal Jr. and Richard A. Jones, do you think the VA is doing an adequate job? Explain your answer.

Chapter 2

1. Large numbers of Iraq and Afghanistan veterans are in need of VA services. Linda Bilmes asserts that VA is ill-prepared to meet this monumental challenge. Jose Riojas maintains that the VA is adjusting and growing to meet the needs of veterans. With which viewpoint do you agree?

2. Erin Mulhall believes that the VA is having trouble meeting the needs of the growing numbers of female veterans. Bradley G. Mayes contends that the VA is up to the challenge. After reading both viewpoints, how do you think female veterans are being treated?

3. Is the VA doing enough for veterans suffering from Gulf War illness? Review the viewpoints of Lawrence Deyton and the Research Advisory Committee on Gulf War Veterans' Illnesses to form your opinion.

Chapter 3

1. After reading the charges by Joshua Kors that the VA is misdiagnosing veterans with post-traumatic stress disorder—and Michael J. Kussman's defense—whose view do you believe is more credible? Explain your answer with evidence from the viewpoints and the authors' biographies.

2. Traumatic brain injury (TBI) is thought to be an emerging problem for veterans of the Iraq and Afghanistan wars. After reading viewpoints by Kelley Beaucar Vlahos and Donna Miles, describe how you think the VA should be handling this dilemma.

Chapter 4

1. What is assured funding and is it the best way to help fund the VA? Review the viewpoints by William A. Boettcher and Henry J. Aaron to form your perspective.

2. Phillip Longman contends that the VA could be the model for reforms to America's current health care system. Nina Owcharenko argues that the VA is flawed and shouldn't be expanded or used as a model. What are your thoughts on the issue after reading both viewpoints?

3. After reading divergent opinions on a new GI bill, by Barack Obama and Steve Chapman, what do you see as the benefits of the bill? What do you see as the drawbacks?

Organizations to Contact

The editors have compiled the following list of organizations concerned with the issues debated in this book. The descriptions are derived from materials provided by the organizations. All have publications or information available for interested readers. The list was compiled on the date of publication of the present volume; the information provided here may change. Be aware that many organizations take several weeks or longer to respond to inquiries, so allow as much time as possible.

American Legion
700 N. Pennsylvania Street, PO Box 1055
Indianapolis, IN 46206
(317) 630-1200 • fax: (317) 630-1223
Web site: www.legion.org

Established in 1919, the American Legion is the nation's largest service organization for veterans. The American Legion provides a number of services to U.S. veterans and their communities, including mentoring kids and sponsoring youth programs; advocating for a strong national security; and supporting policies and programs that help American service members and veterans. One of the organization's most successful programs is American Legion Baseball, an amateur athletic program that imbues sportsmanship and competition in youth. The American Legion is particularly political, actively lobbying for pro-military and pro-veterans policies. It publishes a wide range of publications for children, veterans, and nonveterans, and these works explore a diverse group of topics of interest. The American Legion Web site also hosts forums to discuss issues relevant to veterans as well as a series of blogs, one of which is written by the national commander of the American Legion.

American Veterans (AMVETS)
4647 Forbes Boulevard, Lanham, MD   20706-4380
(301) 459-9600 • fax: (301) 459-7924
e-mail: amvets@amvets.org
Web site: www.amvets.org

American Veterans (AMVETS) is considered to be one of the leading service organizations for veterans in the United States. One of the most valuable services AMVETS provides to veterans is a network of trained national service officers (NSOs) that are accredited by the Department of Veterans Affairs (VA) to advise veterans on compensation issues and assist veterans on procuring prompt action on compensation claims, at no charge. AMVETS also lobbies for effective national defense policies, services for homeless veterans, adequate funding for the VA, improved employment and training programs for veterans, accountability for those missing or imprisoned, and flag protection practices. AMVETS members volunteer approximately 250,000 hours a year to visit hospitalized veterans; the organization also offers a number of scholarships to graduating high school seniors. *American Veteran* is the official quarterly publication of AMVETS; the magazine explores issues relevant to service people of all ages. Another source of information on vital veterans issues is the American Veteran blog, found on the AMVETS Web site.

Department of Veterans Affairs (VA)
810 Vermont Avenue NW, Washington, DC   20420
(800) 827-1000
Web site: www.va.gov

The U.S. Department of Veterans Affairs (VA) is the governmental department that coordinates and administers veterans programs, including health services, disability compensation, educational and vocational programs, home loans, life insurance, survivors' benefits, and burial remuneration. One of its most important responsibilities is the VA health system, which supervises facilities that offer a wide range of medical, surgical, and rehabilitative care for veterans. The VA Web site pro-

vides a link to recent congressional testimony, speeches, brochures, fact sheets, official forms, manuals, handbooks,
updates, and videos. The VA publishes the *VAnguard*, a bimonthly magazine that explores issues relevant to veterans.

Disabled American Veterans (DAV)

3725 Alexandria Pike, Cold Spring, KY   41076
(859) 441-7300
Web site: www.dav.org

The Disabled American Veterans (DAV) is a nonprofit charity
organization composed of 1.2 million members dedicated to
improving the lives of veterans by providing advocacy and
valuable services. One such service is the Voluntary Services
program, which coordinates a network of volunteers who provide veterans with free rides to and from VA medical facilities
and work to boost the morale of sick and disabled veterans.
The DAV also represents veterans and their dependents in
dealings over benefit claims with the Department of Veterans
Affairs and Department of Defense. DAV publishes information on volunteer opportunities and annual reports as well as
recent speeches and *DAV Magazine*, which provides in-depth
articles on veterans programs and policies.

Iraq and Afghanistan Veterans of America (IAVA)

292 Madison Avenue, 10th Floor, New York, NY   10017
(212) 982-9699 • fax: (212) 982-8645
Web site: www.iava.org

Iraq and Afghanistan Veterans of America (IAVA) is an association established to advocate on behalf of the troops and
veterans of the wars in Iraq and Afghanistan concerning medical and mental health programs, improving VA care, addressing the needs of female veterans, and educating veterans about
educational and vocational opportunities. IAVA also strives to
provide a forum for veterans to come together, become em-
powered and active in the veterans community, and support
legislative policies that help veterans of all wars. IAVA publishes op-eds, success stories of veterans, press releases, and

speech transcripts on its Web site as well as links to recent media appearances of IAVA spokespeople discussing issues relevant to veterans. The IAVA Web site also features a blog and offers forums for veterans to discuss issues and connect with other veterans.

National Association for Uniformed Services (NAUS)
5535 Hempstead Way, Springfield, VA   22151
(703) 750-1342 • fax: (703) 354-4380
e-mail: info@naus.org
Web site: www.naus.org

The National Association for Uniformed Services (NAUS) is a veterans organization that advocates for the benefits of all uniformed veterans, soldiers, and veterans' families. NAUS also works to influence U.S. government policy on national defense issues; support political candidates who advocate the interests of U.S. service people and veterans; educate and influence media perceptions and coverage of military issues; and help soldiers and veterans navigate through the VA bureaucracy to get the best treatment possible. The NAUS Web site links to valuable VA forms, instructional manuals and guidelines, health care providers, and other essential resources. NAUS also provides a weekly update on veterans issues, including new policies and programs for U.S. soldiers and veterans.

National Coalition for Homeless Veterans (NCHV)
333 1/2 Pennsylvania Avenue SE, Washington, DC   20003
(800) VET-HELP • fax: (202) 546-2063
e-mail: info@nchv.org
Web site: www.nchv.org

The National Coalition for Homeless Veterans (NCHV) strives to end homelessness among veterans by lobbying for better policies, promoting collaboration between veterans organizations and government agencies, and educating the public and policy makers about the growing problem of homelessness among U.S. veterans. NCHV acts as the resource center for a national network of community-based service providers and local, state, and federal agencies to provide emergency and supportive housing, food, health services, job training and placement assistance, legal aid, and other services to veterans. The NCHV Web site provides essential links to instructional materials, applications to relevant veterans programs and grants, guides to service providers, and fact sheets on issues that are pertinent to U.S. veterans. It also publishes a monthly e-newsletter that covers upcoming events, funding opportunities, and new programs and policies.

National Organization of Veterans' Advocates (NOVA)

1425 K Street NW, Suite 350, Washington, DC   20005
(877) 483-8238
Web site: www.vetadvocates.com

The National Organization of Veterans' Advocates (NOVA) is an association of lawyers and non-lawyer practitioners who receive special training to effectively expedite veterans' claims through the VA bureaucracy. NOVA advocates are fully cognizant of veterans benefits law and can argue a veteran's case at every stage of the appellate process to best procure the appropriate benefits. NOVA also advises veterans on changes in benefit law and apprises clients of new benefits. NOVA provides a wide range of information on veterans benefits, veterans benefit law, and the claims process. NOVA offers a variety of links on its Web site for individuals looking for any information on the claims process.

Service Women's Action Network (SWAN)

PO Box 1758, New York, NY   10156-1758
(212) 683-0015
e-mail: info@servicewomen.org
Web site: www.servicewomen.org

The Service Women's Action Network (SWAN) is a nonprofit human rights organization with a mission to improve the welfare of U.S. servicewomen and veterans. SWAN works to educate the public on issues that impact female veterans; lobby for policy reform; create empowering and healing community programs; and offer a place for female veterans to network with one another and find resources they need in their daily lives. SWAN publishes information on its Web site on the plight of female veterans, upcoming events, new programs and policies, and links to useful resources.

Veterans for Common Sense (VCS)
900 Second Street NE, Suite 216, Washington, DC   20003
(202) 558-4553
Web site: www.veteransforcommonsense.org

Established in 2002, Veterans for Common Sense (VCS) is a nonprofit organization that was formed to advocate for veterans programs and policies and to lobby for issues impacting the freedom and national security of the United States. In the area of veterans, VCS has been active in encouraging veterans to get post-traumatic stress disorder (PTSD) treatment as well as disseminating information about health care, rising suicide rates, and the problem of homelessness among U.S. veterans. The VCS Web site provides links to key news stories, commentary, and reports on issues relevant to veterans. VCS also publishes fact sheets on issues related to the Iraq and Afghanistan wars and VA health care and reform, as well as recent speeches and congressional testimony of VCS staff on related veterans issues.

Veterans of Foreign Wars of the United States (VFW)
406 West Thirty-fourth Street, Kansas City, MO   64111
(816) 756-3390 • fax: (816) 968-1149
e-mail: info@vfw.org
Web site: www.vfw.org

Made up of 1.6 million members, the Veterans of Foreign Wars of the United States (VFW) is a combat veterans organization that is chartered by the U.S. Congress. Members must be U.S. citizens and soldiers or veterans of the U.S. military. They must also have a record of military service overseas during a conflict and decoration with an expeditionary medal or ribbon. VFW lobbies Congress for improvement in health care and benefits for veterans and provides aid to veterans with their disability claims. VFW publishes *VFW* magazine on a monthly basis, which offers in-depth studies of veterans issues, stories about veterans' experiences, and information on VA services and programs. VFW also publishes *Checkpoint*, a bimonthly newsletter that covers news and recent events relevant to veterans.

Vietnam Veterans of America

8719 Colesville Road, Suite 100, Silver Spring, MD   20910
(301) 585-4000 • fax: (301) 585-0519
e-mail: communications@vva.org
Web site: www.vva.org

Vietnam Veterans of America (VVA) is a congressionally chartered, nonprofit veterans organization dedicated to advancing the well-being of Vietnam-era veterans and their families by advocating for issues important to them. The VVA works to change the public perception of Vietnam veterans; investigate America's missing and imprisoned soldiers; ensure full access to quality health care for all veterans; support the war veterans of recent conflicts; and lobby for research and treatment for disabling injuries and illnesses incurred during military service. VVA publishes the *VVA Veteran*, a bimonthly magazine that provides in-depth coverage of issues relevant to Vietnam veterans and their families.

Bibliography of Books

Nathan D.
Ainspan and
Walter E. Penk,
eds.

Returning Wars' Wounded, Injured, and Ill: A Reference Handbook. Westport, CT: Praeger Security International, 2008.

Milly Balzarini

The Lost Road Home: Post Traumatic Stress Disorder (PTSD) and the Psychological Effects of War on Veterans and Their Families. Rogers, MN: DeForest Press, 2008.

Mathew H.
Bradley, ed.

Veterans' Benefits and Care. Hauppauge, NY: Nova Science Publishers, 2009.

Thomas W. Britt,
Carl Andrew
Castro, and Amy
B. Adler, eds.

Military Life: The Psychology of Serving in Peace and Combat. Westport, CT: Praeger Security International, 2006.

Allen Clark

Wounded Soldier, Healing Warrior: A Personal Story of a Vietnam Veteran Who Lost His Legs but Found His Soul. St. Paul, MN: MBI Publishing Co., 2007.

Patricia P. Driscoll
and Celia Straus

Hidden Battles on Unseen Fronts: Stories of American Soldiers with Traumatic Brain Injury and PTSD. Drexel Hill, PA: Casemate, 2009.

Sylvia J. Egan, ed.

Post-Traumatic Stress Disorder (PTSD): Causes, Symptoms, Treatment. Hauppauge, NY: Nova Science Publishers, 2010.

Nader Elguindi   *My Decision to Live: Story of the First U.S. Naval Officer to Earn His Submarine Qualifications with a Prosthetic Leg.* Poughkeepsie, NY: Hudson House, 2006.

Charles R. Figley and William P. Nash, eds.   *Combat Stress Injury: Theory, Research, and Management.* New York: Routledge, 2007.

Aaron Glantz   *The War Comes Home: Washington's Battle Against America's Veterans.* Berkeley, CA: University of California Press, 2009.

Martin Kantor   *Uncle Sam's Shame: Inside Our Broken Veterans Administration.* Westport, CT: Praeger Security International, 2008.

Yvonne Latty   *In Conflict: Iraq War Veterans Speak Out on Duty, Loss, and the Fight to Stay Alive.* Sausalito, CA: PoliPoint Press, 2006.

Harry Lee and Edgar Jones, eds.   *War and Health: Lessons from the Gulf War.* Hoboken, NJ: John Wiley & Sons, 2007.

Phillip Longman   *Best Care Anywhere: Why VA Health Care Is Better than Yours.* Sausalito, CA: PoliPoint Press, 2010.

Ilona Meagher   *Moving a Nation to Care: Post-Traumatic Stress Disorder and America's Returning Troops.* Brooklyn, NY: Ig Publishing, 2007.

Christopher P.   *The Military Advantage: The*
Michel and Terry   *Military.com Guide to Military and*
Howell   *Veterans Benefits.* Annapolis, MD:
                    Naval Institute Press, 2009.

Don Philpott and   *The Wounded Warrior Handbook: A*
Janelle Hill   *Resource Guide for Returning*
                    Veterans. Lanham, MD: Government
                    Institutes, 2009.

David W. Powell   *My Tour in Hell: A Marine's Battle*
                    with Combat Trauma. Ann Arbor,
                    MI: Modern History Press, 2006.

John D. Roche   *Claim Denied!: How to Appeal a VA*
                    Denial of Benefits. Washington, DC:
                    Potomac Books, 2009.

John D. Roche   *The Veteran's Survival Guide: How to*
                    File and Collect on VA Claims, 2nd
                    ed. Washington, DC: Potomac Books,
                    2006.

Martin Schram   *Vets Under Siege: How America*
                    Deceives and Dishonors Those Who
                    Fight Our Battles. New York: Thomas
                    Dunne Books, 2008.

Raymond   *War Trauma: Lessons Unlearned, from*
Monsour   *Vietnam to Iraq.* New York: Algora
Scurfield   Publishers, 2006.

Brian Trappler,   *Modern Terrorism and Psychological*
ed.   *Trauma.* New York: Gordian Knot
                    Books, 2007.

Lawrence J.
Webber and
Katrina L. Webber

The Complete Idiot's Guide to Your Military and Veterans Benefits. Eds. Tom Stevens, Nancy Lewis, and Jan Lynn. Indianapolis, IN: Alpha Books, 2008.

Index